AF506696

WOODS and WATER

Walking New York's Nanny Hagen Brook

MICHAEL INGLIS

Illustrated by GG Kopilak

Published by Hickory Nut Books
Pleasantville, New York

Print ISBN: 979-8-9881079-0-3
eBook ISBN: 979-8-9881079-1-0

Printed in the United States of America

Contents

One

Deepest January

When we try to pick out anything by itself,
we find it hitched to everything else in the universe.

—John Muir, *My First Summer in the Sierra*

A DARK GREY DAY and I'm at the confluence of three little streams as they flow down into Nanny Hagen Pond in the village of Pleasantville, Westchester County, New York State. The wind dances through the beech leaves still on the trees across the stream. The clouds threaten rain. This quiet spot on the edge of suburbia and the countryside is peaceful. The stream trickles gently by. Little bits of foam, the occasional twig and leaf drift pass. The water is beautifully clear.

You can see all the way to the sandy bottom. Around me this incredible cattail, bulrush, reed, and bramble wetland.

The stream is about 10 feet wide and two feet deep at this point. A few yards upstream two smaller streams merge. The one from the south flows gently; the one from the north, the Nanny Hagen Brook, much more strongly as it has come from a larger watershed.

In the middle of this community, the Catskill Aqueduct brings water to New York City from the Catskills to the Kensico Reservoir. Above the aqueduct, high tension powerlines go from Indian Point downstate. This 40-acre piece of land is an edge ecosystem, tucked in between houses and developments. In this stretch, there are wetlands to the north and south of the aqueduct. Adjacent are wooded private properties, a small village park and pond, and a wooded town park.

Later we'll look at the whole stream, but for now, let's focus on this wild middle. Here, birds seemed louder, animals bolder, and nature more clamorous. Liminal yet rich, teeming with life and energy.

This time of year, it's all brown here. The tops of the trees backed by the scudding clouds are silver browns. Some bark is dark steel, some rich chocolate. There are red browns, pink browns, and amber browns. The mugwort, dried and dark, waves as the wind picks up. Grass underfoot has a little green in with the grey, hanging on in the middle of winter.

The cattails' cylindrical heads are bursting apart. Dark brown outside seeds give way to the soft downy, fluffy white insides. The seeds take off in the wind. Some of them catch up against neighboring plants in the area. As I hold up a clump of seed in the air, thousands, no tens of thousands, of seeds from this one bulrush float away. One will settle, and where it settles it may germinate and there will be a new bulrush.

The stems stand eight to 12 feet tall. They're anchored firmly into the wet soil. Their thin leaves veer out from the stems, most of them cracked over at crazy angles with edges sharp and clean. The leaves are hollow and have a structure similar to an aircraft wing with connecting tissues to give them strength. The stems are strong and whiplash back and forth in the wind. They wait with infinite patience for the wind to take the seeds.

The seed heads of the wild carrot also have a fantastic shape. Three- to four-foot stems are topped with beautiful star-shaped structures. The white umbels from last summer are long gone and the stems have since curled into themselves. They have dried into stars. In the cold winter air, they open again and release seeds. Carrots grow wild on this patch of ground. They are biennials: during the first-year, food is stored in the white tap root and in the second year all that energy goes into seed production; in this roaring wind the seeds get picked up easily and fly away.

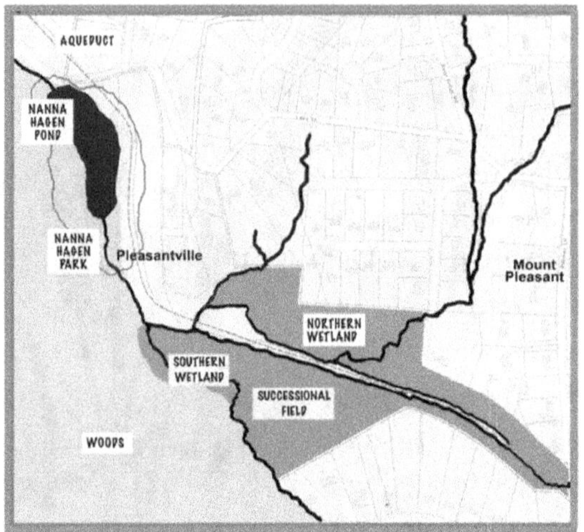

The Nanny Hagen Brook flows down into the Northern wetland.
It then makes its way east and is joined by three small tributaries, before
flowing into the Nanna Hagen Pond (Nanny Hagen is the Anglicized
version of the Dutch Nannahagen). A successional field is on higher ground
to the southeast, woods to the southwest.

To the north side of the aqueduct is a swampy area of about five acres. In the middle the trees that grew there — maples and tulip — have mostly died; it's too waterlogged. Their trunks still thrust bravely into the sky, pointing to the blue. At the top, all the branches like so many little fingers point too. There are maybe 200 fingers on each tree. Isn't that great: they have fingers, we have fingers and they are all pointing into the blue.

A most disturbing sight at the eastern end of the path: the stream has silted up a little into a small pond and its exit has become a collection point for plastic bottles. There must be over 500, maybe 1,000 plastic water bottles, bobbing in this one small group. I will bring a garbage bag over the next few months and start to clean them out. It may take a few trips. Along the path I've also seen an old plastic chair, a deflated balloon, and other detritus that has seeped its way into this pristine and delicate ecosystem.

The phragmites reeds, both to the north and south of the aqueduct, stand tall. Twice, three times my height. Twelve to 15 feet tall and at the top they have magnificent plumes. As the strong wind bends them over, whips them back and forth, their seeds too fly away.

Taking a track to the south of the aqueduct leads you to a higher piece of ground. When I first walked this area 20 years ago, this was a mown and well maintained acre or two of grass. It has since reverted to wild, succession has set in. Saplings are growing and the invasive mugwort has replaced the grass. Along the path my feet crunch in the ice and frost. Frozen leaves give way satisfyingly underfoot. A little depression in the path is iced over and as I step on it, it cracks like a gunshot, breaking under my weight.

As I walk back west on this southern side I pass underneath an enormous tulip tree that has crashed over on its side. This noble must have fallen many years ago as almost all its bark has peeled off leaving the grey wood pitted where ants and termites are at work. They have established a magnificent colony, cutting honeycomb tunnels throughout the fallen trunk. Judging by the number of holes, they have been hard at labor for many years.

This brings you through the beech, oak and maple woods to a gorgeous four-acre wetland. The feathers of frost begin to creep across pond and bog. There is a slight layer of ice on it now. I stand quietly in solitary awe. Getting down and looking more closely at the ice on the edge reveals a thin sheen of grey, yellow, green oil on the surface of the water. This is so disappointing to see. Someone must have discarded some oil upstream, perhaps in a driveway, and it has flowed down to here. A little oil, now frozen into the ice.

A bit further along I come to a remarkable branch that is shaped like an arch. One part of it has all the bark peeled off, but the other half has a fantastical pitted pale orange lichen growing on it. While the lichen feeds itself, the bark peels and decays. On the sunny side, green furry moss is growing well in deep January. Unveiling itself to the sun.

Around me slate dark-eyed juncos dart about on this raised piece of scrubland. They're certainly eating well on all the seeds that are available. I come across some coyote scat. The first is dark, black and moist with no bones or hair indicating that the meal was of internal organs. The second scat is dark grey and mostly deer hair. As it continued to feed, the meal got worse! The juncos however eat well, foraging here in a large group. Flitting through the shrubby thickets, scratching the leaf litter for seeds with their pinkish bills. In a few weeks these birds will be off north to Canada's boreal forests to breed.

It has been dry this January and the water levels are low. As I push my way into the wetland to the north I come across a beautiful cherry with three main trunks. One of them has been seriously damaged by a white-tailed stag rubbing the velvet off his antlers a few weeks ago. On one side, the deer has ripped through the cambium to the heart wood underneath. The total damage is about 20 inches in length and stretches halfway around the trunk. It continues on one of the other trunks, but I think this tree will survive. I will keep my eye on it through the year.

Following the deer path, I come to the spot where the Nanny Hagen Brook comes into the wetland. It flows under a small bridge over the driveway of a house. It broadens out to 12 to 15 feet, then narrows, splits and meanders as it pushes into the reeds. On the right bank you see some ochre soil, colored from iron oxides. And then a small patch of weed, which is bright green on this sunny January afternoon.

Twenty-five little song sparrows rush in to feed. Pecking for seed that has fallen off the goldenrod and mugwort. As I approach they all blast up into the air and fly off. These birds are small but stout and plucky. With thick streaks of russet and white on their heads and chests they flit about with a downward push of the tail feathers. They are delighted by their song, as am I.

To the south, a small brook comes into the wetland at a higher elevation and cascades 20 feet down a waterfall. Today it has ice shards reaching out over the top of the flowing water. Below, the water fills a deep pool situated directly underneath a large power pylon and then flows into a small valley before pushing west. As I walk back my eye catches a desiccated carcass of a small black-capped chickadee. A sharp beak and an unseeing eye. All dried up. Dead and gone.

It's a little colder this morning. The hoar frost is about, silvered and crystallized with joy and delight. As I walk east on the aqueduct the rising sun filters through the trees. The ground sparkles, mostly white, but here and there, red, green, yellow and violet. I step more carefully on the twinkling jewels. The dried stems to the sides lost their own leaves long ago, but this morning they have grown new ones of ice.

The ice that has frozen on the wetland is about an inch thick, with patches that are crystal clear and smooth, and patches that are ruffled and white. I gingerly step out; it holds my weight. Suddenly, nine geese honk and wheel overhead looking for water to land on. No water here, just ice. They fly off south, probably to the Kensico Reservoir.

To the side of the path I find three puffballs. They look like little leathery jacket potatoes, but the insides are all brown. As you open one carefully, the green brown smoke of spores drifts out. I sit drinking in the quiet. My eye is drawn to another fungus growing on a small branch. The parchment vellum leaves spread out from the base. Soft and pliable as I write a word of thanks on them.

The sun slants in from the southeast and I'm on a spit of dry land looking into the thick coat of ice. Bulrushes and grass tufts poke up here and there. Frosted bubbles embedded in the ice and, under it all, thousands of leaves wave as the current moves west. Two rusty red cardinals flit by, not as bright as they are in the spring, but nonetheless enjoying the space.

The beaver has been busy. About 3o yards up from the pond he has built a small bank den on the north side of the stream. He blinks at me as he swims by into the pond, a wake behind that paddling tail. Little brown nose, glinting eyes, and tucked in ears.

Snowflakes muffle and mute. A peaceful quiet descends on the land. Broken suddenly by eight mallards taking off like a shot from the stream, squawking loudly as they fly to the east in a sensuous curved line.

At the eastern end of the land is a small valley where the stream from Palmer Lane enters. Most of the year this is impassably swampy, but we are in the midst of a dry January. I follow the deer track into the hawthorn thicket, one out of three stems rubbed raw by the white-tailed stags. The damaged stems are a cherry garnet. Further on the milkweed pods have all burst, but one or two still have their seeds, packed in so cleverly. Each rust brown seed has a two-inch silky tail, strands of bright white fluffy cotton, and there must be 5oo seeds packed in each grey pod. A broad-winged hawk swoops out and spirals up into the sky. Happy hunting.

Three skittish white-tail deer are ahead on the path. As I near them they leap over the stream off into the undergrowth. White upright tails flash against the brown trees. There was a lot of rain last night and the stream around the beaver den is dark, full and reflective. Drops fall from the branches and as they land waves appear and move out in ever expanding circles. The reflection of the trees and clouds shimmers delightfully. Then another drop, shimmer; then another. The geese and mallards on the pond noisy. Heads down, tails up as they feed off the bottom. Further upstream the water burbles away. In the smaller tributary to the south it is only tinkling. But tinkling sweetly.

A bright sunny morning and the goldenrod sways in the wind. Its tiny fluffy white seeds release and take off. The mugwort seeds are different, little, round and brown, most still fastened securely. I've found the remains of a deer carcass that was killed by coyotes. It's in a thicket of weed, brambles and porcelain berry and there is little left. Only a few bones: a bit of ribcage, a jawbone, a mess, but it's kept the coyotes and others going. It wasn't a big deer, an adolescent probably.

I sit down from the beaver den watching the water flow into the pond. A blue sky, pillowy silver clouds and the sun are reflected in the water. Silvery shimmers, trunks and branches and you can look right down into the endless blue sky. Under the sky are rocks and leaves. The perfect delicate branches in precise detail. A luminescent otherworldly quality. And now the sun comes out in between the crack of two brown smoke clouds, a fiery disc in the water. Around the orb of the sun a glowing red cloud.

The birds greet me happily this morning, all is right in their world. Cardinals are out in force, tails up and down, looking at me. I'm looking at them, we're all enjoying this warm spring-like day in the middle of January. At the southern edge the wetland abuts a slight escarpment. An oil can, twelve old tires, some scrap metal have been tossed over the side as if to get rid of them. But they haven't gone away. Still here.

On a slightly higher spot, three white pines stretch their branches to the sky. A glorious pale blue with puffy white clouds. These are the only conifers in the area. Next stop, a young beech grove. There must be over 200 beech saplings from about five to 20 feet tall. They are all huddled next to each other. Closer inspection reveals that the two larger trees have red, oval-shaped fungal fruiting bodies up the trunk. This is beech bark disease. In response the trees have put out clonal root suckers. Scale insects have pierced the bark and fungi have invaded. In response the trees have root suckered and put up new saplings.

To the north the little stream has stars of ice on its surface. Each star radiates out from a leaf or a pebble, the initial freezing point. Then the crystal grew in the cold. The stream gently pushes into the dense bank of reeds. Tall brown and vertically glinting in the sunshine, water seeping in at their feet.

There are a lot of brambles among the bushes. In the winter sunlight the stems are a bright deep plum which contrasts so strongly with all the greys and browns behind them. The rich, vibrant plum cascades out sharp with thorns. I find two whitened deer leg bones in a patch of grassland. The ends have been chewed over, licked clean, the marrow all sucked out. Bleached bright in the sun. A little frost on them, icicles in the decaying lacey collagen matrix. These bones are probably from a deer killed two years ago.

I'm now at the point where the Nanny Hagen Brook flows into the wetland. When the aqueduct was built, a channel for the stream was made around the north of the property, but it has overflown and eroded its bank and instead seeps southwest. The channel is now mostly dry with lots of dead trees lying horizontally over it. The water flows instead through the wetland. Geese honk as they fly overhead.

At the top of the rise to the south, two old yellow birch trees stand sentinel. The smaller is an intriguing character. From the ground up to seven feet, half the trunk has been blasted out by lightning. The inside is all charred out. After its injury the tree has grown a new root which comes around in front of the damage. From the top of the strike two big branches grow well. The poor old tree is remarkable, still upright, dignified and alive. I give it a hug and well up. This tree so represents our world: beaten down, struck by lightning, but hanging on.

Six turkeys forage ahead of me through the woods to the south. With their iridescent green-brown purple feathers, this group all females. I quietly try to keep up with them, but they move quickly and noisily. They must be talking about the acorns and other mast. There's lots of it about. Perhaps they're also discussing where to roost tonight.

Two broad-winged hawks wheel and screech above as they look down. This patch of land, this hiding place of cosmic glory, has become a home. A place of deep contemplation and grace. We have an illusion of separation, but a moment here challenges us to remember all of who we are and how connected life is.

Two

Snow

It was a winter such as when birds die
In the deep forest and the fishes lie
Stiffened in the translucent ice, which makes
Even the mud and slime of the warm lakes
A wrinkled clod as hard as brick.

—Percy Bysshe Shelley, *Summer and Winter*

FEBRUARY ARRIVES with a light dusting of snow. Across the top of a big fallen
tree are coyote prints. The clever dog ran
all the way from one end of the trunk to the
other. The coyote was on her balance beam and
having fun. In the afternoon sun the surface of
the frozen wetland is a cloudy aquamarine blue.

A big snowstorm descends. It snows for
almost two days and we have about 18 inches.
Two days later I manage to slog my way up to the
aqueduct and am met by fox prints. I've seen her
a few times. With splendid red coat, bright eyes,
pricked ears and easy gait she amazes me, a perfect hunting machine. As a couple are courting
now, the male is pungently marking nightly. You
can still smell it now, so does she. Red fox, wily,
adaptable and an excellent predator. Foxes live
in social groups of two to six adults, but forage
independently. In the late night I sometimes hear
them shriek to each other.

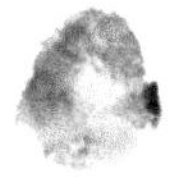

The boulders in the stream all have their
white fluffy hats on. They look so round,
soft and billowy, as the water rushes on by.
One of them has small bird tracks on top.

It is a real trek to get into the land with all this snow. But the deer tracks tell me they and the birds don't have the same problem.

I know this small piece of land. Its rich vibrancy. I know it now in the depth of winter, I know it in the heat of summer. I have walked every path and looked in each nook and cranny. I've watched the birds and tracked the animals. It breathes in and out with the water. It is solitude, a gift, safe, enchanted and grace-giving.

While walking along the trail I think back to when the Catskill Aqueduct was built. Planning started in 1906 and work on the 92-mile long tunnel was completed in 1916. The Schoharie and Ashokan Reservoirs in the Catskills were built next, feeding over 600 million gallons a day to the Kensico Reservoir and on to New York City. That's nearly 7,000 gallons a minute under my feet.

The work in this area was completed in 1912 according to the marker on the cut for the Nanny Hagen Brook which crosses over the top of the aqueduct. The tunnel is 14 feet wide and 17 feet tall. What a feat of engineering. The Kensico Reservoir was also enlarged at that time, burying the small village of Kensico which was about four miles south of here.

Snowing again, so quiet and muffled. The only sounds: the hiss and crackle of the high-power electric lines above, and the downy woodpecker drumming in the distance. Exhilarating with his flash of scarlet on the back of his head. Tap, tap, tap at the trees, he must be finding insects, which is great. Lunchtime.

Another eight inches of the fluffy stuff fell yesterday. All is clothed in white. The trees have snow on their branches and the plants are decorated in icing.

The sensitive fern with dark chocolate fronds is dotted around the wetland. The sori, spore producing receptacles, are clustered like beads on a necklace, alternating as they move up the stem, giving this fern its common name — the bead fern. This place is a balm for a weary spirit, allowing me to sink back into the earth; the stream and I are one beat of the same pulse. The world insists we are what we do, but contemplation here encourages me to simply be.

I've never seen a weasel in the wild up here, but today I spot weasel tracks running parallel to those of a squirrel. Both sets show that the hind feet land on the same spot as the front feet. The weasel's tracks are larger and spaced further apart. I'm sure the weasel got dinner. They eat up to a third of their body weight daily. This is one of nature's perfect checks and balances, perhaps explaining why they have such a bad rap.

The deadly little carnivore is dressed in winter white this time of year, with a tail tipped in black. Weasels molt twice a year. From brown to white in late fall and back to brown in spring. In its winter white they are known as ermines. The fur of royalty. Pelts sell for around 20 dollars on eBay. I think one set of tracks is more noble than any ermine cloak.

In the forest all is quiet. According to their tracks, the deer are still around. Not much else is. The silent trees wait patiently for spring in the hazy afternoon sunshine. We could learn a lot about patience from the trees. Along with patience, nature is so honest. Nothing has a mask on, trying to be something other than it is.

The cold is biting this morning. It grips at my nostrils and tightens them in its vise. I plough my way into the wetland and forest to the south. The woodpecker still taps in the distance, and three crows fly by. I'm at a little deer crossroads. Three or four tracks cross at this one point. Even the deer are having a difficult time getting around, their hooves sinking about 9 inches into the snow. My hooves are sinking about 12 inches, so I'm in more trouble than they are.

A little further in I see bobcat tracks. Four toes with a big pad behind. These confirm a few sightings that I have heard about, but not experienced myself. Wonderful to have this cat back here.

The wild mulleins have pretty much shed all their seeds. Such upright stately plants. Five to six feet and gorgeous yellow in the summer. Now a dark brown with golden edges, this stem still stands tall and erect. The mullein is native to Europe, but was introduced as a medicinal herb. Unlike many of the other plants around here, it is not aggressively invasive. The creamy white fluffy goldenrod seeds are also still hanging on. The bulrush heads look pretty tattered as their seed blows off in great clumps.

I creep upstream from the pond and the beaver is out in a small patch of water that is not iced over. He swims downstream a little. He has made a slide in the snow where he gets to gnaw on the bark of a fallen log. His burrow is well protected now with all the snow on top of the sticks and mud, the entrance still underwater. But he sees me and ducks back into his burrow. A shame, as I would have loved to spend more time together.

The thick snow protects not only the beaver. Underneath you can sense the world of mice and voles hidden from the eyes of the circling hawk. The fallen leaves mulch down and give up their nutrients to the soil. The decomposers, fungi and bacteria, are still active. Those nutrients can then be taken up by the roots of the plants and trees and the cycle can continue in spring as buds start to shoot. A great transformation as the land winters.

Blue jays and cardinals disturb the crows. The bulrushes are tattered and the reeds haphazardly tilted over by the wind. We are in the last stages of winter here, mid-February, and the snow a thick, heavy, wet cloak.

As the end of February approaches, it warms a little. With rain on snow we get banks of thick fog. The mourning doves call to each other with their lament. They have such lovely colors: blue around the eyes, and a pale salmon-peach belly with a flash of purple.

The viburnum buds awake and start to grow, although they won't bloom for another eight to 10 weeks. So have the lilac buds. I cut some of the wild forsythia and bring it inside. This will force the buds to flower. The yellow of spring in my house in a few days. Nice.

Two turkey vultures fly out of the woods and start to circle and gain altitude on a thermal. Higher and higher, then they drift above me to the south. Looking down at me and wondering whether I'm edible or not. They move off to the south. Each night 60 to 80 of these magnificently ugly birds roost in a grove of white pine near my house, to the west of here. They come back home each evening.

The clouds part in the east and the evening sun sets all the world aflame. Crashing in, it lights up the world in its glory. What transcendent beauty. The golden shafts in the reeds contrast starkly with the dark ominous clouds above.

On this dark snowy morning 24 mallards startle me out of my reverie. They explode from the stream to the right of me in a great beating of wings and honking. Magnificent, the energy and the drama.

Now in late February the sun warms and the snow melts. The streams flow with great vigor. Spring is around the corner. The water gushes over the rocks and down. Some of the small plants over the water have ice hanging at their tips. I take my seat by a small eddy. The water hits a rock and bubbles up back around in the quiet. The bubbles form and pop as they make fantastic circles. They catch the flowing water and shoot over to the rock. Most make it back again into the eddy. Entertaining themselves in a never-ending and captivating fractal.

The dried-out mugwort, of which there is so much here, still has its seeds on its tips. The sun and snow bleached it from chocolate to pale light brown. Almost white at the tips, darker at the base.

The fox has been out on her regular route again. Her tracks lead down to a bush where she has been diving into the snow, hunting. Maybe she got a mouse or a vole. I hope so.

The beaver has been busy too. His industry is clear from the large pile of chips strewn all around. A little further in he has cut down ten or 12 smaller trees. All that's left are small 18-inch stumps with sharp stiletto points. The felled trees have been dragged back to the den and he is enlarging it well. Home renovation time. He has also stripped a fallen log; the cambium is pretty much the only food available at this time.

More rain, more fog. Under their cover I creep up on three browsing white-tails. Food in winter is woody browse from anything they can find. They startle and I head up the hill to the south. Towards the top I find several depressions in the snow where they had bedded down for the night.

February, a difficult month, is ending. New rhythms pulse all around as the days lengthen. Clear passages make themselves felt, soon growth will begin.

Three

Stirrings of Spring

True solitude is found in the wild places,
where one is without human obligation.
One's inner voices become audible.

—Wendell Berry, *What Are People For*

WITH THE RAIN that we have had, the Nanny Hagen Brook is full, right up to the top of its banks. Three feet deep, six or seven feet across, the water rushes over the rapids. Happy days.

While sitting on a dead log that's tumbled over, I notice two holes drilled into a branch next to me. Almost four inches deep and recently made. Woodpecker has been here and hammered into the core of the wood in search of insects.

The beech buds are lengthening as the clock turns. The old leaves on the beech have just about all fallen off now. The wetland ponds look tranquil, still covered in a thin sheet of ice, but spring is imminent. You can begin to feel it, and it is so welcome.

Chaste winter virgins, the snowdrops, poke up amongst the patches of snow. Three large white petals frame three shorter heart-shaped petals hanging from the stem. The inner three have bright green stripes which lead in to the orange anthers surrounding the yellow stigma. What can give us more hope that we are near the end of winter than the hardy snowdrop? A plant to soften the roughest edges of our natures.

Four mallards paddle quietly by. Two beautifully speckled females and two males with deep green and purple heads. Courtship involves a lot of bobbing and shaking of the heads. These are already paired up, but still occasionally bob as they go. Their bright orange feet paddling hard against the current.

The males of the red-winged blackbirds have arrived to noisily stake out territory. I love how they puff up when they sing. Proud with their red-yellow badges. Deep in the woods the snow still lies thick on the ground, except around the tree trunks where little patches of bare earth show through. Radiant heat from the bark has melted the snow.

The entire northern wetland stirs. The ice has just about melted and the palest shoots of green are visible. Where the brook flows in, daffodils poke up. I'm sure no one planted the bulbs here so these must have sprung from seed. Hundreds of sensuous skunk cabbage spathes grow tall, but not yet unfurling. Maroon, with yellow and brown speckles, or green with maroon speckles. Amazingly, these thermogenic plants, 10 to 30 degrees warmer than the air, melt the snow and ice around them.

Two days later and the cabbages have shot up. Hundreds of them, very skunky. Most still closed, but two have opened to reveal the spadix: a small sphere covered with tightly-packed yellow flowers. Female flowers at the bottom mature first, male at the top later. A dusting of yellow pollen lies on the petals waiting for an insect to carry it on. No insects here yet. We need a few more days of warmth.

I find a big 30-inch red oak that has recently been uprooted. The hairs at the end of the roots still fresh, but now drying in the air. It must have come down in one of the storms recently. Other pillows and cradles show here and there. Shallow depressions near elevated mounds where trees uprooted years ago. Tawny water, with a raw skin collects in this new cradle.

In the main body of the wetland you would hardly believe that the water was flowing. Everything serenely still. As the water slows the sediments and pollutants settle. Roots bind the pollutants: oil and salt, zinc and copper, pesticides, herbicides, fertilizers — all get taken up and to the west the cleaned water flows out in a narrow channel at great speed. What a miracle.

The red viburnum buds swell. They crack and peel on the side closest to the stem as they start to unfurl. At the beech grove, the trees have finally lost last year's leaves. Although one or two stragglers hang on. All the new buds have started to grow, most are half an inch long. To the side of the grove the stream meanders in two loops around a little island with three trees. They rejoin and enter the wetland to the west.

It's a bright and blustery afternoon. The wind a distinct roar in the background. Trees moan and sigh. Talking to each other and the other inhabitants of the woods. All is quiet for a moment as the wind subsides. As it picks up again, the creaking and groaning revives.

On southern facing slopes most of the snow has melted. But in some northern facing or deeply shaded spots we still have a thick layer. The surface froze again last night and it's easy to walk on. The waterfall is deeply frozen around the edges. Half the pond is frozen; the other half open water which glitters in the sun.

A patch of yellow moonglow lichen catches my eye. The moonglow is like paint on the bark. I suddenly see lichen everywhere. Green-grey paint on the rocks below. And then I come across a fallen branch covered from top to bottom in leafy lichens.

Lichen are living associations between fungi and algae, and an interesting model: make me food and I'll give you shelter. The algae, which often thrive on their own, are basically imprisoned in the fungal hyphae. But what colors! In the forest to the south a big limb has come down across the path and is completely covered in the palest aqua-green crustose lichen.

Sitting under a giant white pine I notice that it's dropping clumps of needles. Evergreens drop leaves occasionally. White pine was such an important tree in the history of the colonies. There is a white pine on the Massachusetts Bay Colony charter and on its first coin, the Pine Tree Shilling. These magnificent trees were valued for their height and straightness, so were treasured for masts. Their wood is soft, easy to cut and without knots. In a high wind, it bends rather than breaks. Trees with a diameter greater than 24 inches at 12 inches from the ground were marked with three slashes of the "King's Broad Arrow", an old sign depicting British naval property. The Broad Arrow Policy served to fan the sparks of rebellion. This giant is safe here. Or is it?

All red-winged blackbird males are territorial. They love these reedy wetlands and many here stake out their space. Such a deep inky black, with a lovely flash of red and yellow. This male gives me the beady eye and flies at me. I'm intruding, but then he sees another male and that's a more important tussle. Males arrive back in the spring a few weeks before the females and establishing territories is key to attracting a mate.

The bulrush heads are almost completely bare now. Great clumps of seed fly off in the wind. At their feet the voluptuous curves of cabbages grow fast in the wet soil. Two mourning doves gently nibble at each other's necks as they build a small nest on a branch. Across the stream two sparrows mate. Three seconds and it's done; eggs will be on the way.

A most peaceful early spring morning. The wind has died down and temperatures warm into the 40s. Pussy willow catkins, from the Dutch for kitten, *katteken*, are budding out. Silver flowers as soft as a kitten's tummy. Shining beacons. The snow is melting and the quiet interrupted only by the cardinals, the mourning doves, the blackbirds and the woodpecker in the distance. Time in solitude allows a reboot, access to memories forgotten. This birdsong takes me back to childhood on the Bay of Bengal and the parakeets in the casuarina trees. At present, nothing much stirs but the blackbirds.

Two broad-winged hawks out here hunting. They fly south across the aqueduct and perch on a dead tree limb. Disturbed, they start circling on a thermal to gain height. Twelve, 15 times around each other on opposite sides of the gyre. Then they soar off to the northwest, dark tips on broad wings.

A downy woodpecker meticulously examines a dead tree in the wetland. He starts at the bottom and looks in at each hole as he works his way up. In one larger hole he dives right in and spends a little while checking it out. It could be a possible nest site. Higher up he pops into another hole. Now he's at the top, looking around, then off to the next tree to start giving that one a thorough going over. Diligent and industrious.

Temperatures are moving into the low 40s and rain is forecast for tonight. Amphibians will start their great migration. Spotted salamanders will come down from the forests to the vernal pools.

New green shoots appear on the wild thyme and chives. I remove some brown dead stems to give the new growth sunlight. That will help it along, not that it needs my help. The Japanese honeysuckle vines start to bud out. Little green shoots up and down the vines.

Dark brown fresh coyote scat along the path today tells me that they ate well. I turn the corner and am greeted by a truly handsome animal. This is a big boy, at least 40lbs. A deep rust brown coat. Lots of guard fur, large ears pointed and erect. The eastern coyote looks at me with utter indifference, mixed maybe with a little curiosity. Not much fear, though. He takes a few steps towards the reeds.

Stops and looks back. Then he turns, shakes his head, and takes off into the undergrowth. As nature disappears around us, I treasure these precious meetings more and more. Essence is revealed, each encounter satisfies and heals. Feral is always exhilarating.

Eastern coyotes only came to New York State after the wolf population was decimated by humans. Genetic analysis shows that they have roughly 64 percent western coyote, 26 percent wolf, and 10 percent domestic dog ancestry. Interestingly, records show that they spread into New York from Canada in the 1940s, only arriving in Westchester in the 1980s. Happy here now.

A tiny yellow warbler is flitting about the eastern pond. Four mallards have taken up residence here too. Ducklings on the way. The deep snow is almost all gone. A small patch remains, covered in brown paw prints. Everywhere else the leaves, like pages in a book, lie flat. Around the pond, stems and leaves have dried out, cracked in half and crashed over. New green shoots begin to poke up from below.

As the days warm, insects start to hatch. Bees arrive, clouds of midges fill the air, the birds feed and the skunk cabbages are pollinated. The scent pulls them in to have a look. Across the northern wetland, irises and sedges have all greened up. The water is flowing cheerful clear. Reflections sparkling bright, clean and new. Such a renewal enlivens both nature and soul.

Two more sparrows are mating over the stream. They then flit to the shrubs. Insects hatch, birds gorge and I see the first spider out weaving her web. And — great excitement — I enjoy my first sighting this year of the native eastern chipmunk. The little guy darts along a log and into a burrow. Stripes flying.

Four dawn redwoods stand by the pond. The village has put protective nets around their bases to keep the beaver out. These deciduous conifers lose all their leaves in the fall and have just started budding new ones. How beautiful the ground beneath: delightful cones lie all around, four-sided boxy chocolate ovoids on long stalks. Seeds all gone, the squirrels have been feasting.

With the warmer weather, the beaver has been busy again. He's chopped down two more small trees including a four-inch diameter hawthorn and a three-inch maple sapling and dragged them both back to his den. It's almost five feet tall now, and about 15 feet across. Quietly, I walk around to the back of the den and see that he has taken down a ten-inch diameter, 40-foot maple! Remarkable. It's fallen towards his den, but unfortunately into a tangle of dead trees, and sadly, he hasn't managed to drag it far. So much labor, such disappointment.

The entire southern wetland is alive with spring peepers and wood frogs. As I walk up they all go quiet, so I settle on a log a few feet from the pond and keep still. After a few minutes they start to sing again. Yell is more like it. I can barely hear the airplane above as it comes in to land at White Plains airport.

Shallow, warm and mucky-bottomed, the wetland is about four inches deep. Tan wood frogs, with black masks, scoot about the surface, legs splayed out. Quacking like ducks, they call out as they rush about madly, looking for love. The ripples disturb the reflection of the trees and sky behind. Astonishing to think that these bundles of energy were frozen frogsicles just two weeks ago.

The peepers are smaller; they too are calling to mates. To the left I spot five white-tailed deer gingerly walking past. They look amazed at the noise of the love-mad frogs. Wondering what the heck is going on and how could they possibly be so noisy.

The Canada geese are back on the pond. There are 14 this year. They will be nesting, and goslings will be here in a few weeks. We usually get two or three families. We'll see this year. A few days later and no geese. Very unusual. Perhaps it's the presence of the beaver.

I've always wondered how much water is moving through the wetlands. Rough measurements indicate that, after it leaves the pond, Nanny Hagen Brook has a cross-sectional area of about 3.8 m² and the water is flowing at about 0.9 m/sec. This calculates to a flow of approximately 1,000 gal/sec. Stupendous.

The northern wetland in late March is now a bright green carpet of iris and Pennsylvania sedge shoots. The skunk cabbage leaves spiral up. Iridescence in the sparkling water which flows left, right and then forward. A large collection of pear puffballs grows on a decaying log at the water's edge. Creamy soft and pillowy, with smoky spores on top of white strands of hyphae.

March ends with green on the weeping willows; touches of red on the maples as tasseled flowers bud; and yellow forsythia. Yellow and silver on the goat willows too, as their catkins burst into life. Spring bounty.

Four

Birds and Blossom

sweet spring is your
time is my time is our
time for springtime is lovetime
and viva sweet love

(all the merry little birds are
flying in the floating in the
very spirits singing in
are winging in the blossoming)

— e. e. cummings, *sweet spring*

I'M ON A BIRD WALK with my friend James Eyring, assistant director of the Environmental Center at Pace University. We hear the Carolina wren, "Teakettle, teakettle, teakettle," he says. The white throated sparrow, "Sweet, peabody, peabody." The red-winged blackbird, "Curlewee." Then we spot a tree swallow. A lithe bird with white belly, iridescent blue back and that lovely swallow tail.

Along with the downy woodpecker, we see the red-bellied woodpecker. This lovely beast is black and white on top, with a red crown and nape, and pale red-white belly. Pileated woodpecker is here too. We hear the deep, rolling drum in the distance. This is a big bird, about the size of a crow, but with white on the neck and a flaming red crown. James hears yellow-bellied sapsuckers and northern flickers too, and points the flicker out on the grassy bank. This bird is a large woodpecker with marvelous scalloped black spots on a tawny breast, flash of red behind the head. He notes, "These birds like eating ants on the ground."

Two black-capped chickadees, "Fee-bee-ee, fee-bee, hey-sweetie." These little grey birds have white bibs and black caps and feed on the stems of the reeds. They check us out, such curious little birds.

We find a praying mantis egg sac, an ootheca, on a branch by the stream. After the cannibalistic mating in the fall, where she eats her partner, the female laid around 200 eggs in this tan little sac. They'll hatch soon.

"Listen," says James, "Tsee, tsee, tsee, tsee, tsee, tsee." A small high-pitched golden-crowned kinglet announces its presence. This tiny bird has a fabulous crown of yellow and red. We walk to the east end of the land to the small pond. Mallards are here, as are wood ducks. The male, with green and purple crested head and chestnut breast is bold and brash. The female, with warm browns and blue speculum. Wood ducks like cover and we have a lot of that around here with the willows and hawthorns. James notes, "My favorite duck."

Tufted titmouse is here too. This eager little gray bird with bushy crest flits by. Its fast song "Peter, peter, peter" is repeated quickly. An American robin makes a nest, using her wings to push twigs in.

We pass a big ash tree on the edge of the forest. Unfortunately, the emerald ash borer is at work and the tree has been badly damaged. Nobody knows exactly when the iridescent green jewel beetle, which was a native to Northeast Asia, arrived in the US, but it was first detected in Michigan in 2002. By the end of that year around 6 million ash trees were declining or dead. It has now been detected in 35 states and has killed hundreds of millions of trees.

Adults lay eggs in bark crevices and, after hatching, larvae chew down into the wood and create u-shaped galleries that cut off water flow in the tree. This poor ash has an extensive population and great chunks of bark have fallen and lie at its base. A magnificent tree, like so many other ash in Westchester, is now on its way to death. Feel its pain.

A large bumble bee, fuzzy round yellow and black, hovers back and forth. She finds nectar in the mounds of lesser celandine. These pretty yellow flowers are among the first to bloom after the skunk cabbages. This is another invasive. It has been here a lot longer than the ash borer, introduced from Europe in the 1860s. It has some of the shiniest petals in the plant world, produced by oil cells on the upper surface. The petals turn matte at the center of the flower, to help guide insects to the nectar. Its early appearance, and tubers which spread easily, helps it to form thick mats which push out the native spring ephemerals.

I spot some black knot, a fungal gall on a cherry branch. It will release spores one wet and warm day soon. This visible world is only the surface of stratified reality. Layers are there for those who look.

A murmuration of starlings on the grassy aqueduct. This European bird was first introduced in Central Park in the 1890s by Shakespeare lovers. The group decided to bring over every bird the Bard mentioned. The population has taken off and it is now one of our commonest birds. The large flock lifts off in unison and banks down to fresh grass. It's wonderful how these birds gather together, moving as a large mass across the sky. They twist and turn into singular shapes. Apparently, a murmuration forms when one starling copies the behavior of its seven neighbors, and then those nearby starlings copy each of their seven neighbors, and so on until the entire group moves as one.

Three white-tailed deer approach. I stand stock still. Close, and they don't know I'm here. Freed into the present. Time stops. Bliss to be in the eternal now. One scratches the side of her head with her left rear hoof and looks quizzically in my direction. Am I anything other than a tree? Her coat is rough and mangy — clumps of fur have fallen out. This is caused by mites and explains her scratching. She goes back to browsing the forest floor.

These deer damage forests in the region. Large populations have over-browsed the forest understory. In much of this depauperate woodland the only remaining understory shrub is spiky Japanese barberry. This plant was brought to the United States in the early 1800s for gardens, but it now dominates forests in 32 states. The barberry has also been shown to create the humid conditions that encourage deer ticks to thrive.

White-tailed deer are plant-devouring machines. Gone are the spice bushes, the azaleas, the witch hazels, the sweet pepperbushes. Gone are the coneflowers, the woodland phlox, the rudbeckias. Gone are the native grasses and the wild strawberries. Gone are the saplings. And if the saplings are gone, the forest will be gone. As Aldo Leopold said, "I now suspect that just as a deer herd lives in mortal fear of its wolves, so does a mountain live in mortal fear of its deer." All is not well in this forest. I wish the coyotes happy hunting.

On my walk today spiky angelica is budding, the lesser periwinkle, violets and delightful Virginia spring-beauties in bloom. The spring-beauties, a native, are being strangled out by the lesser celandine. But a good number hang on here by the path. Five white petals with pink stripes aglow. The stripes are nectar lines for pollinators which lead to pink anthers and sugar. Spring-beauties are generously sweet and visited by many native bees. The corms, "fairy spuds," are edible too. I don't want to dig one as the flowers are too precious and they feed my soul.

Common dog violets and common blue violets in bloom. The dog violet is a little paler. But it's the masses of cuckoo-flower that catch the eye. Also called milkmaids or lady's smock. Four petals of palest pink. The pinnate compound leaves are a good spicy addition to salads. We also have the cut leaf toothwort, a close relative. And tucked away, Dutchman's breeches, with its filigree leaves and racemes of white flowers. The showy banks lift the spirits.

Nothing is more spectacular than the pink and white flowers of crabapples and cherries. Both star performers in the symphony of spring. Flowers open, anthers hang full of pollen, swaying in the breeze. This cherry is smothered in pink clouds of transient ephemerality, with many petals already on the ground. Days of glory and then gone. Life is an ever-changing series of transitions.

In the southern wetland the cinnamon ferns are just begin-ning to furl up. Next to them two delightful spring transients: the wood anemone and the dwarf ginseng. Anemones are common here, but the dwarf ginseng is a rare delight. About five inches tall, the little white ball of delicate lacy flowers sits above its three leaves. Up the hill, another native Dutchman's breeches with dark lacy leaves and white hanging flower.

A bent, gnarled old willow has fallen over, but is still alive. Branches reach up from the horizontal trunk where it has re-rooted in the wet. Fresh thin and lanced leaves glow. At its feet the four petaled bird's-eye speedwell. Pale blue with darker violet lines radiating out. Great egret, showy white tail and all, lifts off from the reeds. Straight up and then down and out over the water.

A full moon. Bullfrogs croak and the coyotes howl. A chunky black-crowned night heron stands still at the edge of the pond waiting for prey.

The great greening has begun. We are confronted with the good news of fecundity. Leaves bud, canopies green. Flowers blossom and there is an abundance of nectar. Insects buzz. Painted turtles sun themselves on the cracked bulrushes. Dark olive carapace with flash of red along the side. The raft of frogs' eggs has hatched and tadpoles squirm and feed.

Chartreuse cypress spurge lights up the banks. Brilliant yellow beacons that trap the pollinating insects. They are not flowers, they have no petals, no sepals. But at the top of each stem are resplendent bright yellow cyathiums. Invasive plants such as this pretty one push out the natives, leaving us with monocultures: the celandine, the mugwort, the yellow flag iris.

A large striking jack-in-the-pulpit tucked away in the beech grove. Quite the preacher with his exotic toxic canopy. The spathe is strongly ribbed and the three-part leaf stands aloof. This one is putting up a male flower. If all goes well next year it may put up two leaves and a female flower. When times are hard, it will revert back to one leaf and male. This back and forth may go on for several decades.

Jack-in-the-pulpit is an arum, which in Arabic means fire. Beware, cook well before eating the roots, called Indian turnip. To the west of the southern wetland is a small rise of land with the stream to the south. The land is only a foot or two higher, but drier. It is covered in a great array of cinnamon fern fiddleheads. Don't mistake these for the edible ostrich fern. Cinnamon fiddleheads are furry and mildly toxic.

I come across a whole clump of trout lilies. A surprising number in bloom. Maroon mottled leaves and a solitary nodding flower. Six yellow petals in a star, three twisted back and three forward. It only flowers after ten years of digging itself deeper into the ground. Just uphill is a large cracked granite boulder. A carpet of Canada mayflowers fills the crack to overflowing. Each stem with two shiny, oval leaves and the bud. They will flower white in a week or two. In flower now is the bloodroot, red stemmed, with eight big white petals and yellow center. The reddish sap can be used as a dye and gives the plant its common name.

A small silver birch buds out. Serrated leaves splash this corner of the hill in harlequin green. The male catkins sway pendulously in groups of four, the female is smaller, short and erect. Next to it is an alder with similar, though larger, catkins. Clumps of five, soft and furry, sway in the breeze. Sex on display.

On the way home, I end the month by helping a big snapping turtle across the road. When I pick him up he is not happy, hissing and nipping. This one weighs over 30 pounds and what an amazing tail, truly dinosaurian.

Early May, another glorious spring day into which one is admitted and suspended and sent on. Time seems to stop and wait.

The wind gusts for the conifers. The white pines grow fresh candles and at their base new cones. Male cones will release millions of pollen spores. They will drift on the wind and find the female ovulate cones. These ingeniously put out drops of water to catch the pollen. Oaks are also pollinated by the wind, so their flowers are not ostentatious. They too are not trying to attract the wind.

Clouds of insects rise up from the stream as it tinkles happily. Flowering plants often use insects to transfer the pollen from the anthers to the stigma. After landing, the pollen grain germinates and grows down through the style to the ovary where it fertilizes the egg. The ovary begins to grow into a fruit, either dry or fleshy. Seed in fruits will hopefully be eaten and transplanted to a new location. The pollinator turns one into millions.

This pollination pact evolved between plants and insects millennia ago. The Oxford English Dictionary defines mutualism as 'the doctrine that mutual dependence is necessary to social well-being.' Beetles were among the first. Ancient plants such as water lilies and magnolias still use beetles. These plants have thick petals for clumsy beetles. But the beetles are fed and the plant is pollinated. Both benefit. Oh, but could we do the same.

Among the insects the bees are king pollinators. Leaf cutter bees have hairs on their bodies to collect pollen which they then feed to their offspring. Flowering plants produce nectar, an energy dense meal. Pollen is also protein rich and often a good food source for growing exoskeletons. But this helps pollen transfer too. What's good for the insect is good for the plant.

Butterflies are nectivorous with long proboscis straws. But they only tiptoe around the flowers. They really don't get down and dirty in the pollen. Hummingbird moths are the same. Both are nectar thieves, with their long tongues.

Flower shapes are important – open, dish, bell or funnel. Brush shaped maples. The gullet-shaped violas require the insect to crawl right in. Insects perceive colors and patterns on petals as guides to the nectar. Lots of shapes for lots of mouth parts.

The yellow flag iris is all over the northern wetland and they make the insects open the flowers to get to the sugar. Three flowers at the end of each stalk. I imagine myself as an insect arriving on the landing petal to follow the intricate veining, then to push my way under the covering petal. Finally, sweetness. Yellow flag is native to Europe, Asia and northern Africa and was imported as an ornamental in the late 1700s. In the northern wetland the irises have formed a dense monoculture, magnificent in bloom but dense in root. They have pushed out everything but the skunk cabbage and the sedge.

Flowers need to make sure the pollen gets delivered to the right address. So, we have co-evolution of a search image, a reward that lives in an insect's brain. These are learned, some even pass from generation to generation of insect. How the plants have outsmarted the insects!

Canada geese are careful to keep in pairs. They move their necks in watchful ways, around and twined. Mother goose leads the three little ones onto the liquid surface. They launch forth and the male, proud and erect follows. The goslings, soft and tufty down, yellow around the eyes and chest, sandwiched in the middle.

Raccoon slopes slowly down to the woods. She seems a little slow, and isn't usually out in daylight, but she may be foraging longer to support her young. I later find her dead in the woods. She knew the end was close and was just looking for a peaceful spot. Scavengers will come.

I have a walk and talk to Rebecca Policello, Science and Stewardship Coordinator at Teatown Preserve, about the land and its history. Fourteen thousand years ago, this part of Northeastern America was half a mile under the ice. "Large glaciers advanced and retreated," she says, "carving out the valleys and producing striations and grooves in the granite." Long scratches can still be seen in the higher elevations along Bear Ridge, the high ground to the east.

After the ice melted and over the last 8,000 years, this area was a temperate forest with small native populations, who, let's not forget, had their impact. The New Castle Historical Society tells us that Native Americans of the Tankiteke group, of the Wappinger Confederacy, inhabited the area when the first Europeans arrived. At this time the area was mostly deciduous woodland. The middle portion of the stream undoubtedly had numerous beaver ponds, with abundant native wildlife. That all changed dramatically to farmland with Henry Hudson's visit and the Dutch settlers. This land was farmed from colonial times to the mid-twentieth century.

In 1912, it was all change again as the aqueduct was built. Rebecca notes that, "The land is disturbed, but still very diverse. The birds are happy, with cover, food and nesting sites." She goes on to say, "The cover is good and predation levels will be low, but the food quality is also low. The birds love the edge areas but bring the seeds of the invasives." She's noticed that the linden viburnum has come in the last five to 10 years. An ornamental that escaped the local gardens. So has autumn olive. This hardy aggressive invasive is happily colonizing the scrubland. "Look for its red fruits in the fall," she says.

"A lot of the invasives have seeds that are bird transported." Then she laughs, "I don't know where the irises came from. Probably a gardener bought them here."

One happy native holding on is the wild geranium. Pretty purple blue flowers and fragrant leaves. These clever plants will catapult their dried seeds in a month or so. A lovely witch alder with its white bottle brush flower is blooming here too. This plant is native to the south, so its seed must have escaped from a local garden. Probably also brought here by a bird.

The Conventions on Biological Diversity defines native species as "a species that has been observed in the form of a naturally occurring and self-sustaining population in historical times," and invasive species as "alien species whose introduction and/or spread threaten biological diversity." Many of the plants here are invasive. But these new plants support good populations of insects and amphibians. They in turn support birds and small mammals: rabbits, voles, mice, coyotes, deer, beavers, weasel, bobcat, skunks and raccoons.

I find a green spicebush swallowtail caterpillar in a rolled leaf with its yellow and black pseudo eyes. Awe stills the ego and the irksome voice of the self. Surprise repositions us in the world.

Five

Early Summer

To see a World in a Grain of Sand
And a Heaven in a Wild Flower
Hold Infinity in the palm of your hand
And Eternity in an hour.

— William Blake, *Auguries of Innocence*

HONEYSUCKLE BLOOM and feed the night-flying moths. The scent disperses and drifts. Handsome wild roses start to bloom too. Most roses here are the invasive multiflora rose, introduced to North America from Asia. Five white petals, yellow center. It was introduced in the 1800s as a natural hedge, but is now everywhere. Tucked away now and again is the native pink Carolina rose. Five pink petals, with the same yellow centers.

Summer wildflowers bloom out on the aqueduct. A great patch of sulfur cinquefoil. Bedstraws everywhere. Small bladder campions and quite a bit of white yarrow this season. Nice flat top umbels. Red and white clover too — a fantastic bumble bee plant with its composite flowers of long corollas. Darwin noted that bumble bees have longer tongues than honey bees and are the only bees to visit red clover.

A hot, bright early summer morning on the pond. One gosling left, following its mother. A teenager about a third the size of the parent. Growing quickly, but only one remaining. Two red-winged blackbirds descend into the tree next to me and start angrily calling. It's an intense alarm call, "Chak, chak, chak." They don't want me around their young.

The wild bees are out in force. They love the white tipped flowers of the ribwort plantain. Swaying gently as each bee alights. The grassy hill is buzzing. The entire wild hive must be here, the queen close.

Crown vetches grow three to five feet tall at the edges. Pretty white to pinkish-lavender umbels. The vetch was introduced to the U.S. from Europe in the mid 1800s. Widely planted as a ground cover crop, here it serves the purpose of slope stabilizer. Can something be a little invasive? Beneath it is the purple clover and beneath that the white clover. Fragrant and loved by the bumblebees. The young leaves are delicious in salads or soups.

Bittersweet nightshade, five purple reflexed petals with yellow anthers forming a beak amidst the blue forget-me-nots and the yellow creeping jenny. Banks of color, insects and water splashing. Standing sentinel above it all, the magnificent tulip trees are flowering. Extravagant yellow-orange goblets fall to my feet. The largest specimen tree here has a girth of 12 feet, one of the largest trees around here. Truly impressive.

Swallows dart down over the water. We have both tree and barn. Tree with white chests and barn with tawny; both have glistening cobalt blue tops. What aerialists. Swooping up, down and around the water for insects. They've built a cup-shaped mud nest under the bridge. These delightful little birds have come from their wintering grounds in Mexico and Central America. I treasure them and their acrobatics.

The hemp dogbane is widespread with small white flowers just starting to form. Creeping jenny, another non-native, at my feet. Just up the slope, one of our native orchids, pink lady's slipper, unfurls its dark green leaves. A large female eastern black swallowtail, about four inches across, darts into the shady wood.

At the Palmer Lane end of the path, banks of pale blue forget-me-nots. Petals of the palest blue with yellow centers contrast with mounds of glossy yellow buttercups. A patch of yarrow, these with pink umbelliferous heads. Sitting next to them sulfur cinquefoils. Delicate tiny yellow flowers.

A cloud of sparkling jewelwings rises around me. Thin metallic emerald sticks shimmer, hover and dart. Sunshine pouring over. A large black moth, about four inches across, flits into the woods. The harder you look, the more you see. Shafts of light pierce the forest floor. A line of carpenter ants.

An adventure in listening. To the wind, to the stream. It runs fast in a wet June. Toads croak at dusk as they come out from their lairs: a stone, log or pile of leaves.

All is quiet around the beaver den. No sign of activity here, the lone male may have moved on. But my neighbor informs me that he has seven coyote pups under his deck. Mom is away and the little ones creep out to play. Such fun jumping on each other and cavorting around. They are about six or eight weeks old and 15 inches long. Big ears, pointy noses. Some dark, some light. Pups leave the den at eight weeks. Two days later they are gone.

I talk to Chris Nagy at Mianus River Gorge, a coyote researcher. "Wolf pups tend to stay a whole year, but coyote pups tend to leave earlier," he says. "The little ones will stay with the parents for the summer. Sometime in the fall, half of them will disperse. We often see two stay with the parents over the winter and then one of those two will leave in the spring. That last one will help raise the next litter."

Coyote pups often have to travel big distances to find new territory with adequate food resources. Coyotes are omnivorous. Chris says, "They eat deer, roadkill, smaller mammals. But they also eat berries and leaves." Chris references a coyote spotted in Chicago carrying a goose in its mouth. He notes they eat a lot of eggs and goslings. Perhaps that was the fate of the two goslings that disappeared last week.

Chris says that each distinct patch of green space may well have its own breeding pair of coyotes in this part of Westchester. Chris also notes that the coyotes that do best are the ones that are shy of human contact, so perhaps having pups under the deck is not the best for them.

Despite the beauty, the idea of a virgin landscape here in Westchester is an illusion. With the building of the Catskill Aqueduct change came rapidly, led mostly by the invasive species: barberry, garlic mustard, bittersweet, leafy spurge, glossy buckthorn and privet, honeysuckle, common reed, knotweed, porcelain berry and the multiflora rose; and most of all the mugwort. All are now here to stay. Removing them is not a possibility. It's too late, too costly. They also change the microclimate and the soil and will have long-term consequences which we don't yet know.

Silky dogwood, pale forget-me-nots, Deptford pinks and naturalized dianthus grow along the stream. The geese quietly paddle up. The one gosling is now a strapping teenager, but still staying close to its parents. Swallows swoop and dive, gorging on insects that rise up from the water. In the pond, water lily pads grow and the flower buds form. This is a native. Large white petals and prominent yellow stamens will appear on this plant in a few weeks.

Herons visit. The great blue and the green come every year. The great blues have a big nest in a dead tree back in the southern wetland. They fly up and down the brook daily. What a wingspan! You think it must crash as it flies into the woods towards Broadway, but no.

I often see the green heron fishing on the edge of the pond. Once, long ago, I was blessed with the sight of the snowy egret here too. Delicate S-shaped neck and flashing yellow lore — a male in breeding plumage. Black bill and shocking yellow feet. It was under the fresh soft needles of the dawn redwoods by the pond whose trunks flute elegantly at the base.

Along the mowed path of the aqueduct the blue chicory starts to bloom as does the bee balm which attracts the butterflies along with the bees. These tough natives hang in here. A lovely mullein is growing fast. About a foot tall now, it'll be five feet in a few weeks. The American bumblebee, an endangered species, is in and out of the clover. Carolina horsenettle is also attracting them.

The vegetation fills in. I clear the path as I hack my way into the southern wetland. Carpeted with sedges and forget-me-nots. The native tussock sedge glows from within. Light green with blue lights. The cinnamon ferns are up to my chest. Five feet tall with the frogs croaking at their feet.

A small garter snake slithers out. This species is pretty tame and easily picked up. Hello friend. Dark green with a distinctive yellow stripe. She slithers off into the skunk cabbage leaves which are thick and leathery. Lots of holes where the caterpillars have had their fill. The snake will gobble them up.

The buttonbush is blooming with fetching globes of white florets. Underneath some Deptford pinks. The old ash tree that has been attacked by the emerald borer hangs in there. Great heaps of bark at its base. Poison ivy vines snake up the trunk, but the canopy has leafed out. It is not going without a fight.

Relaxing on the boulder in the southern wetland, the frogs croak all around me. To my left and right, glades of New York fern with their spiky fronds, scattered with the eastern woodland sedge. The land is home to the gods, with powers that sustain or extinguish. We have forgotten how to immerse ourselves into the depths of landscape, so we no longer swoop as the swallow, spin with the spider, or sit as a stone.

The arching heads of the grasses nod and waver in the breeze. Making food and medicine from light and water. Rust glints off to the side. The bees are pollinating the sumac flowers which are just coming in to bloom.

July has been so wet. Summer rains swirl and dance. Thick heavy drops arrive with the thunder and lightning. The grass on the aqueduct was cut a couple of weeks back and now, with the rain, new wildflowers push through. The clovers and campions, chicory and carrot. A yellow mullein starting to bloom at its base. The tall five-foot spike has dense groups of five-petaled flowers, a few of which will bloom at a time. Purple wild bergamot pulls in the butterflies.

Lucky to see a little clump of inkcap mushrooms. Such delicate and transient beings. Caps like a parasol, hence the species name, *Parasola*. Tomorrow there will be no trace of these frail fungi.

Towards Palmer Lane the path becomes impassable, the growth of the mugwort and porcelain berry has been tremendous. Miles of strands of vines, all about to flower. This vine has overtopped and is strangling to death so many of the native shrubs and trees in this patch of land.

The porcelain berry belongs to the grape family, Vitaceae, but out-competes the wild fox grape, which can be found occasionally growing along the stone walls. Right now, the berry vines are covered in little white flowers. Come fall, the lustrous, multicolored berries will cascade down drooping vines. Pretty but aggressive.

I hear a frog croak in the pond, enjoying the water. Birds chirping, but it is the smell back here that delights — rich and verdant, the smell of growing plants. A delicate green darner settles. The bulrushes quickly grow their chocolate seed heads. A twelve spotted skimmer sparkles. Twelve brown spots with ten white ones. Why is it not called a twenty-two spotted skimmer?

Bright orange fire on the forest floor: red chanterelles grow beside the path in the woods. These are an edible mushroom, even though the bright red color is a warning. Further along is another red mushroom, the blood red russula, bigger with white flesh, but not edible. Be careful when foraging.

Up on the boulder overlooking the valley, the white wood aster pops up in the same space where earlier this year the Canada mayflower bloomed. The dark stems crink back in the opposite way at each leaf node. Bright green leaves and will be in flower in a month or two.

Back on the path, the wild white carrots grow in profusion. Nestled among them is more orange, the butterfly milkweed. Bright umbels of 20 or so pretty orange flowers. Earlier the pink swamp milkweeds were blooming at the Palmer Lane end of the stream. Both these milkweeds attract the monarchs whose larvae are immune to the toxic white sap.

Hundreds of bees feeding on the white meadowsweet. Great buzzing panicles of densely clustered creamy white froth. Dark red stems, bright green leaves and lots of white flowers. A yellow prairie warbler flits by. Feeding fast after its long migration from Central America.

In the wood I find a clump of ghost pipes. One of nature's strangest plants, it flowers all white on grey-white stems and has no leaves. Nourishment is drawn up through roots which intertwine with the mycorrhizal fungi in the soil — they in turn get their food from the nearby trees. Supposedly a pain killer, but I'm leaving these here.

Birdsfoot trefoil is loved by the bees and the caterpillar of the common blue butterfly. The yellow flowers go on and on. Introduced to North America as a forage crop it's now escaped. As the seeds develop you can see why it was named birdsfoot. Another non-native has naturalized here— viper's bugloss. Blue flowers with purple flecks climb the stem. This plant, like the skunk cabbage, exhibits protandry. The male parts, with nectar, open the day before the female parts, which lack it. The plant fools the bees who visit anyway. The female flowers then put everything into producing seeds.

More white flowers, this time on the sweet pepperbush. Hundreds of little flowers on erect racemes. Orange anthers and cloyingly sweet fragrance in the warm humid summer air.

Time stands still in the shimmering heat. Presence is required. As presence is offered, eternity opens up, past and future disappear. Graced insights in these gifted moments of freedom.

Six

Insects Buzz and Fizz

As imperceptibly as Grief
The Summer lapsed away …
Our Summer made her light escape
Into the Beautiful.

— Emily Dickenson, *As Imperceptibly as Grief*

A LATE SUMMER MORNING, cooler, a slight chill in the air. The purple loosestrife and the goldenrod are in full bloom. Banks of purple offset by banks of yellow. A muskrat scoots down the side into the pond. The waterlilies are out and a frog on a pad hops off. She doesn't want to be breakfast. The muskrat forages in the reeds instead. Then she stops, sits and holds up her four little fingers. Sniffing constantly, little whiskers twitching.

Swallows still skim the water. Diving down and round, and catching the insects rising in the early light. Circles round my head, mercurial birds, lovely tails. The bark on the river birch peels to reveal a salmon skin. The rusty brown seed heads on the phragmites sway in the breeze. Chicory, carrots and clover blooming. Monarchs and swallowtails all over the joe-pye weed, the hemp dogbane and the bee balms. This wild bee balm has prolific lavender flowers and aromatic leaves. A hummingbird moth is feeding too. All of connected life is talking with the wildest music. Just listen.

Native wild cucumber vines intertwine up and over each other. The bright green leaves are similar in shape to maples. The tiny white flowers are all in bloom and smell divine. Look for the spiky seed pods in fall.

Yellow-orange jewelweed complements the purple deadly nightshade. Behind that the red of the morrow's honeysuckle berries; under it all the lesser stitchwort. Five white petals so deeply lobed that they look like ten. Happy bees drinking in the nectar.

A patch of woodland sunflowers stand radiant on strong vertical stems and a goldfinch swoops in to eat the oily yellow seeds which are a source of carotenoids for their feathers. Courtship season is now in full swing and these seeds are helping males around here look their best.

A juvenile milk snake suns on the rocks. Alternating bands of white, red and black. One of our prettiest snakes absorbing the heat and warming up.

Cicadas moan and fizz in the treetops. They've all gone up there to attract each other and, after mating, the females will lay eggs in slits they have cut into the bark. Down below a little mountain laurel bush, which had pink flowers in the spring, now has dark green leaves in the summer. Used by Native Americans for utensils, it was called spoonwood.

The fruits, or pomes, of the red chokeberry hang in great clumps. Bright, almost orange, with black sepals and not the first choice of birds. Further up the hill is the black chokeberry, whose fruits are almost gone. The birds must find these less astringent. Next to it is a sweet pepperbush, with, as you guessed, a spicy aroma.

Under the distinctive shaggy treebeard, so many hickory nuts. I love the bark of this tree, and what a nut — buttery and sweet. The brown fleshy husk peels off leaving a smooth ivory brown nut. Roast them. The white oaks also produced a bumper crop of acorns this year, but not the red oak. One would imagine they might be synchronized. Fresh bright green nuts on pitted brown stems. Lots of good food.

At the Palmer Lane one small tributary moves down through Pheasant Run Park. In this wood the grove of ancient beech has been devastated by the new beech leaf disease. Forty to 50 trees here, ranging in size from around six to 36 inches in diameter, are all affected. The leaves are crinkly and dark and many trees are seeing significant canopy dieback. Really suffering. I'm not sure if they are going to get through another year.

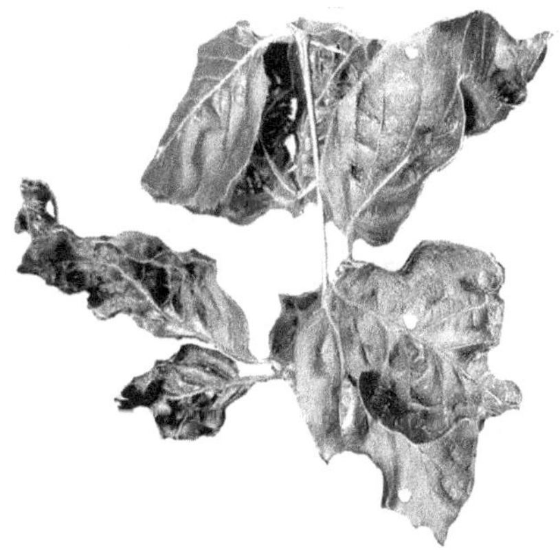

Beech are some of my favorite trees. The dense shade is lovely in this heat. The mast is rich in fat, and squirrels, mice, voles and shrews all love beech nuts. The larger carnivores: weasels, raccoons, striped skunk and bobcats, all depend on healthy populations of these small critters. The loss of beech will be devastating.

The silky dogwood fruits are here. The yellowish white flowers of May are now dark, dusky blue drupes. Song birds, rodents and the white-tailed deer love them. The staghorn sumac shows off its bright red fruits too. These will keep many creatures going late into winter.

The underground world makes itself visible after a strong rain last night. The white hyphal strands of fungi stand out clear on the ground. Mushrooms, their fruiting bodies, pop up. These fungi are the foundation of the forest. They link all the trees. Human actions are fraying and breaking these wild connections. Respectful relations must be maintained with the animals, plants and the land itself. This is the only way to ensure our communities' health.

Tired after a long walk, and my favorite boulder welcomes. Supports. A direct gesture. Ducks call, cicadas chatter, and time almost grinds to a halt. Now I can converse with the clouds, and fly with the birds over the enveloping earth.

Patches of the native common evening primrose are in bloom. The fragrant, bright yellow, four petaled flowers open at night, closing by noon the next day. This native plant is host to the pink and white primrose moth; it times its adult flight period to the blooming. And of course, the delicate moth is as nocturnal as the plant. Tall meadow rue shows itself. Delicate leaves and bright white flowers. Moths will be here tonight too.

The bats are out this evening. The small caves and the shag bark hickory are good summer roosts for the little brown bats. Their populations have decreased in the last 10 years from white nose syndrome. Hundreds used to fly out every night, now only a few. The white fungus grows on the noses of the poor creatures. It's believed to have originated in Europe and was first detected in Albany in 2006. Since then it's spread throughout North America and killed tens of millions of the cute critters.

At night the owls come out to hunt. Screech owl, barred owl "who cooks, who cooks for you" and great horned owl "who's awake, me too". We have all three in these lovely woods. The coyotes join in, howling at the gibbous moon.

Walking down the aqueduct surrounded by butterflies. A pale-yellow clouded sulphur, and a darker orange sulphur, which is a darker yellow. Further on there's a bright orange and black monarch, the colors a warning to predators. Monarchs are toxic to predators as they store toxins from the milkweed that they've ingested. I've also seen its great mimic, in similar colors, the viceroy. Clever, all that protection without any effort. A wild indigo duskywing darts up and down, hopping onto flowers to feed.

A beautiful fall morning, escorted by two floating monarchs and the chatter of the crickets and my friend Andy Reinmann, an ecologist at City University of New York. We have a clear-eyed discussion about the invasive species: "I guess the unsurprising part was the extensive growth of invasive species in the disturbed land along the aqueduct. That's what takes over."

"Native species," he says, "have a whole suite of other organisms that co-evolved with them. What makes the invasive species so problematic and so successful is that while the natives have to deal with pests and pathogens, the invasive plants don't."

Invasive species make up a large percentage of the herbaceous plants in this corridor. One native, the white wood aster, hangs on. And blooming now. Pretty with clumps of bright white flowers on crinkled red stems. Seven or eight white petals, and orange centers. Bees are still busy pollinating the goldenrods and their close cousin the silverrods, white flowered goldenrods.

Andy loves the quaking leaves on the bigtooth aspens as they flutter in the breeze. Doing well in this successional field. Twenty years ago, this was a grass field. Now perennials, shrubs and small trees have moved in. We also discuss the age of the trees in the woods to the south. "About 70 years old, so that area was not forest in the 1940s," he surmises. The stone walls through the trees delineate edges of the old fields.

Two painted turtles bask on a log. I ask Andy if the rare box turtles may be here. He notes, "They need quite a substantial area of upland forest habitat next to the wetland, so maybe." But I haven't seen any.

Can we rethink the management of these areas? Andy notes that we are "fighting the natural trajectory of nature. Every year we stop succession in its tracks, and that provides opportunity for the invasive species to establish themselves again. Once they are as well entrenched as they are here, it's very difficult for the native species. Also, mugwort and porcelain berry are species that grow rapidly and have a high capacity to withstand frequent disturbance."

We have unwittingly displaced the native species and now wonder why we are exiled and separated ourselves. As Wendell Berry noted, "Nature…has more votes, a longer memory, and a sterner sense of justice than we do."

Seven

September Storms

You crash over the trees
You crack the live branch—
the branch is white,
the green crushed,
each leaf is rent like split wood

You burden the trees
with black drops,
you swirl and crash—
you have broken off a weighted leaf
in the wind,
it is hurled out,
whirls up and sinks,
a green stone.

— H.D., *Storm*

THE MONTH OF SEPTEMBER begins with Hurricane Ida. After pummeling the Gulf Coast, she made her leisurely way up to New York. Lake Street was completely underwater. The forecast called for heavy rain for two to three hours late that night. Nothing prepared us for the record intensity. Six inches fell over the course of the night, with more than three inches falling in one hour.

Temperatures have increased globally by nearly 2°F due to man-made industrial emissions. That's the heat equivalent of 4,000 Hiroshimas daily. Warmer air holds more water vapor. As Ida moved across the hot Gulf of Mexico, easy evaporation strengthened the storm from a Category 1 to a Category 4 in two days. Once the water is up in the air it will come down. It came down here last night. The morning reveals the destruction.

I come out to a bright and sunny day. But moving water is as solid and as heavy as concrete. Flash floods last night up and down the brook. They moved boulders, ripped and scarred the ground, and uprooted plants in many places.

The Nanny Hagen Brook, a tributary of the Saw Mill River, ends its life just south of Exit 27 of the Saw Mill Parkway at an elevation of just under 250 feet. About 20 feet wide and a foot deep and flowing well. Up the banks: debris. Stripped vegetation indicates the water was eight feet deep at the height of the storm last night. Looking upstream under the railroad tracks are bits of cars, wood, a headlight, a rake broken off at the handle, a McDonald's coffee cup, and plastic bags and bottles. All trash that was swept downstream.

For its last half mile, the brook is hidden away behind industrial buildings and under roads. What could have been the centerpiece of the area, its greatest natural feature, has been confined and hidden. But nature does not like to be confined. An entire wall was swept away as the brook flooded Franklin Ave., Marble Ave., and Broadway. This area has flooded three times in the last 20 years: Hurricane Floyd in mid-September, 1999; Irene in late August, 2011; and Ida last night, September, 2021. Each of these storms was considered to be a 100-year event. Three 100-year storms in 20 years.

The brook is restrained to a culvert as it moves down from the football field, ironically named the Water Field. This soccer pitch was under eight feet of water last night. Moving north, the stream makes its way through a small gulley, then traverses the golf club and makes a right turn under Broadway. During the storm this was the location of some of the worst flooding and damage. The 12-foot deep channel along Lake Street was completely filled and the street itself flooded. Water that used to run freely did so again.

In a prior era, the village constructed the swimming pool building on top of the stream. Whose idea was that? As expected, the four-foot cistern that channels the water under the building was not large enough. The water ripped up fences, filled the pool with mud and moved on.

How did our beaver fare in the storm? Well he's still here and the den is in good shape. I have a talk with Westchester Parks' curator of wildlife, Dan Aitchison, about our beavers. I ask him how many we have, "There's a lot of beavers in Westchester. But it's not studied and counted." "So, in the hundreds?" I ask. "No, more than that, in the thousands." This is wonderful for an animal that was essentially wiped out.

It has been estimated that before the arrival of the Dutch in 1609 there were millions of beavers in New York State. The settlement on the tip of Manhattan was established by 1614 and the City of New York proudly put a beaver on its shield. However, the next 25 years were tragic for beavers, because their pelts were valuable. By 1640, except for a few colonies in the Adirondacks, the beaver was extirpated, hunted to near extinction. Legislation was passed in the early 1900s to protect them. By the 1930s, upstate beaver populations were thriving. We have one here now.

I first saw our beaver in the late fall of last year and I'd like to know where it came from. I ask Dan about beavers in the Bronx River watershed, which is adjacent to the Nanny Hagen Brook watershed, to the east over Bear Ridge. "I do goose work on the Bronx River every year, from Kensico Reservoir down to the Bronx, and I have not seen any recent evidence of beavers." But that leaves the river north of the reservoir. It wouldn't be surprising. "Beavers move both upstream and downstream when dispersing, and there may be beavers on the Saw Mill River too."

"Juveniles disperse when they are two years old, either in the spring or fall," Dan says. Some studies have shown that they can move up to 15 miles if they have enough time. He goes on, "Let's say this guy was a spring dispersal, he could have been travelling all summer. They can't set up a home where other beavers already have colonies. And they're not going to set up shop unless they find a place with food and habitat."

I go on to ask Dan to describe the process of the juvenile setting up shop. "At the beginning, juveniles will build what's called a bank hole den, a scooped-out hole in the side of the river bank." I note that it didn't take this guy long to then build his big den. Dan laughs, "It doesn't take them long. You have to remember they have nothing else to do all day." I'm secretly pleased that this beaver has made this brook his home.

The main priority with winter coming is to build a home and collect enough food resources. Our beaver has achieved that beautifully. The bank den is now 15 feet long, six feet wide and high. A veritable hall.

He has now started to build a dam across the stream from his lodge. I ask Dan is this the next logical step? "There are a number of reasons beavers like to elevate water," he says. "Firstly, it provides protection for their home. Secondly it allows easier acquisition of food resources. Water provides buoyancy. They can thus move their food and building materials around more easily. Another reason to raise water is to make a food cache in the water for winter which our guy has done. Finally, it's their nature, it's just what they do."

Beavers eat fresh wood, not the bark and not the dead heartwood, but the cambium layer in between. "The green stuff," says Dan. "That's why on their lodges and dams you see these white, completely stripped sticks. They're also eating aquatic vegetation."

I ask Dan about the future of our lone beaver. "Will it stay on our stream?" I ask. "I'm not convinced it will. It may, but it may not," says Dan. "It's been there about a year and it hasn't found a mate." Indeed, it hasn't. I didn't see it over the summer and so I ask Dan if it may have gone looking. He doesn't think so. "They don't really do that." "So, how's it going to find a mate," I ask. "It will be waiting for another one to come down the stream."

That seems pretty unlikely to both of us. Now I'm thinking this wasn't such a good move for our beaver to set up shop here. While we have a lot of beavers in Westchester, most of them are to the north, not down here. "I'm not sure if another one will find its way here," says Dan. He thinks it may move on. "Another factor that could push it to move out would be a limitation of food resources." The village has put wires around trees. It's relatively common for juveniles to move on. So, enjoy this guy while we have him.

Just down from the pool, the stream abuts a large wood where a baby sassafras has germinated and is growing well. Such big bi- and tri-lobed leaves. Further in are larger trees, the dark purple fruits an important food source for many of our native birds. The bark smells of cinnamon and the leaves of lemon. Delicious.

Back in the northern wetland, plants were scoured away. Sand and dirt, pebbles and rocks were deposited 20 yards from the stream bed. The water has recontoured the land, changed the path of the streams; new gullies have been formed. Great clumps of irises tossed aside. The water must have been five feet deep in here; discolored lines in the vegetation show the height. Huge pressures and forces have altered the land.

In the southern wetland, much less damage. This area is only fed by the small stream from the south. The damage done commensurate with the size of the watershed.

There were strong thunderstorms again last night. They must have been associated with wind microbursts as four trees came down. One twisted right out of the ground. Water has scoured out the paths in the woods leaving leaves piled up against the rocks and roots. In dappled sunlight, the stream is full and rushing gaily.

The shagbark hickory nuts all came down in the storm. A lot of them have burst out of their shells. Green and black on the outside, a quarter-inch thick shell which snaps into four symmetrical pieces releasing the light brown nut. The small mammals will be pleased with this windfall: Eastern chipmunks are good at gnawing open the shells, and even little mice will work the nut until they get inside. The nuts are a favored food of squirrels, who of course eat them before and after they fall. Apparently, turkeys swallow nuts whole and grind them in their gizzards.

In the large granite slab, the crack that was filled with mayflowers in spring is now filled with white wood asters. No sign of the mayflowers, they've all died back. It's now the asters' turn to shine.

The sun's path bends to the south as even it seems compelled to try on new colors with the changing of the season. Rich displays of reds, orange and purples light up dusk in the ever-shortening days. Plants now put all their effort into fruiting. This process, the last stage of reproduction, ensures the next generation. Many fruits have bright colors and sugary tastes thus attracting animals who will unwittingly aid in seed dispersal.

Late September and the grey milkweed pods pop open. Seeds burst out and fly off. A green pod, however, is covered in the black and orange milkweed bug. The same colors as the monarch and giving the same warning: I'm not edible. On this plant there must be 200. Some small nymphs along with the larger adults. These bugs, like the monarchs, also migrate south for the winter.

The porcelain berry at the eastern end of the wetland has clambered over everything, making a bold attempt to take over this world. The beauty of the berries is only skin deep. They are a poor food source for our birds. The dazzling blues and purples, resembling miniature birds' eggs, are the reason this vine was brought here in the 1970s from East Asia. Those horticulturists, with a penchant for the gorgeous fruits, had no idea that they had unleashed an invader of epic proportions.

The heads on the phragmites are grey, bushy and a foot long. Golden brown in the evening light. Seed will fly off in the winds to come. There is a native species of phragmites, but the reeds here are non-native, growing in dense clumps 12 to 15 feet tall. All the same, serving a purpose of food and shelter for our birds.

Low clouds scudding to the horizon. The last of the swallows prepare to leave. The trees, too, are getting ready to say goodbye to their leaves, having dropped all their fruits.

Witch hazels' yellow spiky flowers appear as the bush drops its leaves. Sweet and zesty. Its forked limbs were used as divining rods. "Wyche" is the Anglo-Saxon word for bend.

At the end of the aqueduct, banks of jumpseed among the chickweed. Dark leaves with spiky white flowers. White and pink. Seeds will be jumping soon. Great bunches of blue-white panicled asters. Goldenrod turning. Soon all will be brown and grey.

The cottontail rabbits are out this evening. Bronze and silver. I've seen over eight in this little patch. They must have a big warren underground. For safety they spend most of the day down there. The females may even be having their eighth and last litter of the year. Proverbially prodigious. They see me and bolt back to the hole.

Is that a thrush I hear? No, it's my favorite amphibian. The spring peeper is calling. This somewhat perplexing event is happening in October. What are they going on about? The shorter days, the cooler temperatures, and the increasing rainfall are similar to spring when these frogs become active. The male sex organs develop from late July to early September. By this time females have already formed eggs. Because they breed as soon as they defrost in the spring, they may just be getting ready or they may just be teasing.

Up the wooded hill to the south, two dark ferns stand out — the straggly marginal wood fern and the clumpy Christmas fern. Both these native ferns are evergreen, a few remaining splashes of color.

Walnuts have all fallen in the winds. The green husks smell a lovely lemon when rubbed together. Remove the green hulls, but beware the black ink, phenols in the hulls can irritate as well as stain. Washed, dried and laid out, they'll be ready to crack and eat in a week.

The Department of Environmental Protection, New York City's water corporation, has been busy on the aqueduct. They are cleaning a bacterial microfilm from the inside and they have come through with a bulldozer and graded land close to Palmer Lane. This has made access much easier. It's also run roughshod over all the invasive plants growing here. No doubt they'll all grow back quickly.

The ten huge beech, to the east of the southern wetland, all more than 36 inches in diameter, have lost their leaves in the storms. Beech leaf disease has hit them hard this year. These have curled, crinkled, died and fallen. I don't think that they will be back next year. We lost all our chestnuts and elm, then we lost all our ash. Are we now to lose all our beech?

At the end of the month I revisit the southern part of the stream close to the Saw Mill River and find that the plants are still coated with mud from the hurricane's floods. The stream runs clear now and a number of small darter fish, with their split dorsal fins, flick here and there. That's encouraging, a sign of clean water.

The light has changed too: it's cleaner and now slants with the earth's tilt. Bright red fruit of the winterberry contrasts with the dark leaves as the sun sets.

The goldenrods down here are all blooming too. This is such an important native. More than 100 caterpillar species feed on them. These in turn feed our birds and bats. Birds also eat the seeds. A variety of mammals: rabbits, voles, mice, muskrats and groundhogs eat the plant, too. And don't forget the beetles and aphids. It feeds them all.

Eight

The Great Changing

Nature's first green is gold,
Her hardest hue to hold.
Her early leaf's a flower;
But only so an hour…
So dawn goes down to day.
Nothing gold can stay.

—Robert Frost, *Nothing Gold Can Stay*

R AIN, HERON and fox today. The great blue heron fishes at the side of the stream. Walking delicately, cleaning and preening her feathers. She shakes out her wings and a few feathers fly off. Now down to the serious business of eating. Long sharp beak darts into the water. Picks up, tosses out, darts in again, picks up a morsel, swallows. She stands quietly, tall. A little raft of mallards around her.

Orange fox flashes out onto the path, sees me and veers back into the woods. Long bushy tail streams out behind as it dashes up the hill. White tuft at the end, over the ridge and out of sight. Good-bye. Fox was as lively as rain.

The tree of heaven is chockful of seeds. Great clumps hang down. Native to China and Northeast Asia, this was first planted by colonists in Philadelphia looking for quick air-conditioning: a fast-growing exotic shade tree.

This tree employs nearly all the invasive toolkit. It has high seed production; so many samaras on this tree. The seeds are viable in many soil types. It reproduces sexually and vegetatively. Cut it down and root suckers will appear — a many-headed monster. White-tailed deer find it unpalatable, and, after they fall, the leaves leach out a toxic substance called Ailanthone which helps the tree outcompete neighbors. Leaves emerge earlier in the spring and stay green longer in the fall; thus it produces more sugars than its competitors. Altogether a formidable arsenal.

Interestingly, tree of heaven is the best host to another newcomer, the spotted lanternfly. One invasive brings another, this one potentially much more destructive. It came from China and was first detected in Pennsylvania in 2014. It is now spreading up and down the East coast, though I haven't seen it here yet.

Tree of heaven competes with the native black gum, a tupelo, and with the native sumac. Here our tupelo looks good. Many shades of yellow, orange, bright red, purple and scarlet on the same branch. The sour attracts the birds, what a delight.

Another toxic plant, white snakeroot blooms nearby. This is native to North America but was found to be toxic when many thousands died of milk sickness after drinking milk from cows that had eaten the plant.

As the strength of the sun fades with each shortening day, the blaze in the trees only burns brighter and the few leaves left on the dogwoods glow red in the evening light. Arboreal kaleidoscopes gleam with treasure, each leaf speaking bliss to me. Nuts fell, and now the leaves. Crunch underfoot.

Nature comes to life as we live in the middle of it. We are creatures too. Listen to the voices of the animals and trees. As they talk to us, I wonder if we have ever listened at all.

A late October sunny day. Burnt orange, acid yellow. The crickets chirp, and the dragonflies flit over the stream. A praying mantis is still busy. This one is huge, nearly seven inches long. What a splendid beast. There is a native mantis, but it is much smaller. This is a Chinese mantis, imported with plants from China. Long, green with astonishing eyes. Perhaps the mantis will get a dragonfly.

Brown leaves fall in waves as the woods ease into winter. A huge American sycamore leaf settles down in front of me. A gift from the mottled grey giant. Fall is gathering on the ground. The carrot seed heads curl into brown, soon to be grey, stars.

There are infinite forms of exquisite life here. Plants and animals, with diligence and devotion, follow the seasons with regularity. I delight in the colors of the changing and yet lament the greater changing. As temperatures rise species at various levels in the food chains respond differently. This may well result in our ecosystems being driven out of sync.

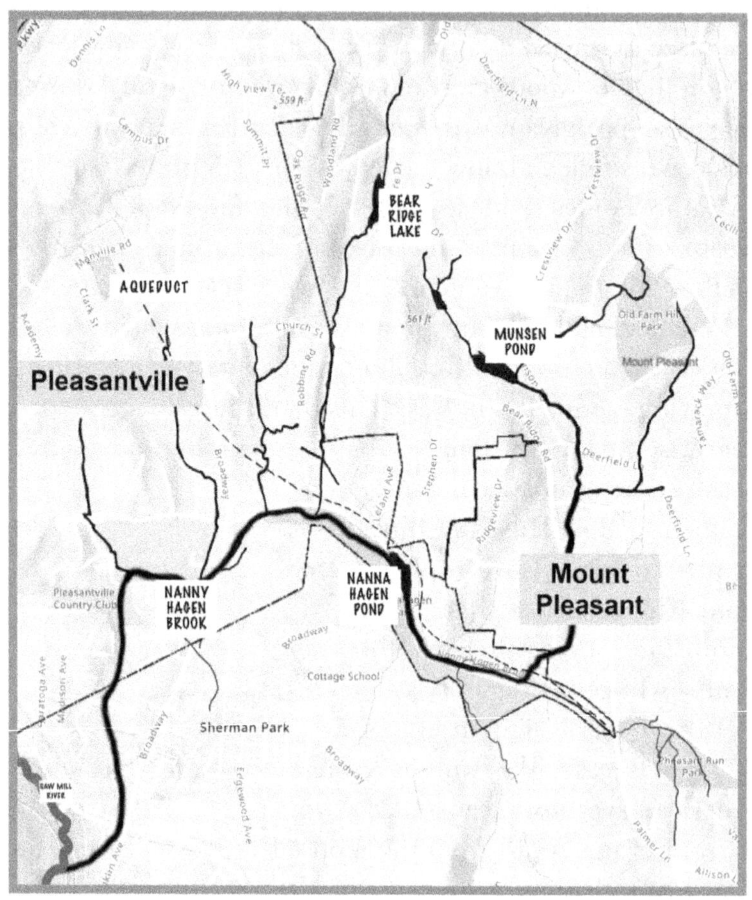

The full watershed of the Nanny Hagen Brook

At the eastern end of the wild wetlands lies Palmer Lane. Across the lane lies Pheasant Run Park. Two small streams flow down through the Park, merge and go through a culvert under Palmer. This park abuts the aqueduct as it makes its way up to Valley Road and down to the Kensico Reservoir. There are three of these little parks in the headwaters of the Nanny Hagen Brook. This one, Old Farm Hill Park and Mountain Trail Park to the north of Bear Ridge Lake. The lower reaches of the brook are in a fairly narrow valley, whereas the upper portions fan out into a large bowl with these three parks at the higher elevations. I spend late autumn exploring these upper reaches.

Pheasant Run Park runs parallel to Pheasant Run Road up to the ridge. Over the ridge, water flows down into the Kensico Reservoir and the Bronx River watershed. Mostly beech trees with an occasional maple, this park was created with this subdivision in the 1970s. This area and that to the north of Bear Ridge Road were farms at that point. With beech leaf disease this park is teetering. Will half the trees here die in the next two years? What impacts that will have on the other creatures here is yet to be seen. Big change is afoot.

The beaver has been busy at the top of the pond. He's strengthening his bank den and starts to build a dam in line with his den entrance. Logs stretch half way across the stream. Smaller branches, twigs and leaves are caught in the current. He's also building up his food cache for winter by dragging short branches and sinking the cut bottoms in the mud close to the entrance to his den.

We've had a delayed fall this year. It hasn't been getting cold at night yet. The average night temperature in October was 52°F. Only a few leaves have started to turn. Suddenly in early November the nights start to get colder. This will trigger the deciduous trees to drop their leaves. The winged burning bush has started to turn a bright crimson. Another pretty invasive brought from Northeast Asia as an ornamental shrub. Flashes of this pink-red gleam through the understory.

Bursting red, white and black, the rose-breasted grosbeak is gorging on the nannyberries. Underneath, a dark vole is harvesting too, running with a full mouth down to its tunnel. Put on fat now, winter will be hard. Stash all the food you can. There's plenty here.

Walking through the fall woods, fill your nose with the incense of fallen leaves, the mustiness piles up in banks of orange, yellow, red and brown. As Walt Whitman said: "After you have exhausted what there is ... what remains? Nature remains."

Goldenrod still blooming in waves. At their feet a first-year mullein with big furry leaves. I love the whorl of silvery grey. This will come into its own next year with its yellow spike of flowers. Great blue heron still fishes in the reeds. It's starting to get cold, will she soon leave for winter?

The fruits on the buttonbush turn red. Pretty white flowers in the summer have been pollinated by the butterflies which this bush attracts and now the fruits will feed the birds. Any nuts that fall to the ground will be gobbled up by the mice. The frost is on the thick piles of brown leaves. Little intricate crystals have grown on their backs. Water rises off the pond as the sun strikes. Mist dances, lifts, twists and rises. So delicate, so fine.

A bald eagle dips down, all muscle and speed, swoops overhead and down the hill. As the eagle disappears I notice a big broad-winged hawk, sitting with large shoulders, watching carefully. Her perch, a branch in the dead ash tree. So many vines make a home in this tree too. As I walk down under she keeps her steely eye on me to make sure that I'm not trouble. "Hello, big girl, hello." There she goes: First of all, swooping down, then after a second up to the next branch she finds in the wood. I'll follow her into the shade.

A northern catalpa, also known as the cigar tree, hides along Bear Ridge Road as the brook makes its way up to Munson Pond. A lovely native tree, still dark with green leaves. Earlier in the year it was covered in clumps of big white flowers with yellow and purple lines. It's now hanging heavy with two-foot seed pods: huge cigars!

Munson Pond gets its name from a Mr. Munson who owned the Munson Steamship line. This was a farm pond on his property here, with an ice house. Early maps indicate Munson owned most of the land around here. A Mr. Drieser farmed all of the land to the west up to the Bear Ridge. Now it's all residential lots.

The dawn redwoods have started to drop their needles. Brown clumps on the ground. Resinous and piney. The weeping willows grey and yellow as their leaves also fall. The tulip trees – once a resplendent gold – are now all bare. Flashes of red and pink euonymus.

I again spot the great blue herons fishing in the weeds. Surely, they must fly south for the winter soon. The quaking aspen leaves are bright yellow and the sugar maples put on their show. I admire the uneven coloring of this tree. Some leaves yellow, some orange, and some still green. The range of these native trees is slowly moving north as the climate warms.

Changes in timing with the late fall create huge problems for birds and insects and the plants that nourish them. Out of sync with each other, one no longer feeds the other.

Our ecosystems have evolved over millennia as tightly knit choreographed performances. Climate change is altering this, and not for the better.

Now that we are into late November, a real chill at night turns the Norway maples yellow and brown. Most trees are bare but these still shout out, "Here I am, look at me." The goldenrod seeds are all fluffy grey and white now, the gold a distant past. A large branch has fallen from one of the dying beech at the northern end of the forest.

The southern wetland is all still. A few chirping birds. A clouded sulfur butterfly, probably the last time we'll see one this year, accompanies me. The water quietly flows under the pinks of the euonymus. Carpets of leaves lie underfoot, soft and brown. Sycamores, oaks, tulips, gums.

The purposeful beaver has brought down a really big tree this time, a 30-inch diameter maple. He's worked on it a while, bite by bite over many nights and felled it in the direction of his den. Last night he chewed the smaller branches and these he bought to his food cache. Some of the larger branches he has dragged into the water a little downstream from his bank den and started to make a dam.

Drifts of orange-red winterberry holly, an important food source for the robins. The red stems of the viburnums and dogwoods come into sharp contrast. Lots of food for the birds here — many Asian linden viburnum with red clustered drupes. These have root suckered to make deep thickets, outcompeting our native arrowwood and maple-leaf viburnums. There are a few of these native viburnums left with their little black drupes and a few remaining dusky pink leaves.

Tiny spades of skunk cabbage begin to emerge. New growth just before winter. The changing seasons herald constant dancing movement between growth, death, and here, welcome rebirth.

I'm startled by a pheasant blasting out of the tall grass. Pheasant are not native to the U.S., but apparently European and Asian ring-necked pheasant were introduced here as gamebirds. Some hybridized pheasant are still around.

Wild deer, fat on summer fruits, walk by. The orange setting sun in the western sky disappears. The sky turns inky purple and the waning crescent moon hangs to the south. In the dark and quiet, the beaver comes out. Surprised by me, he slaps his tail, disappears underwater. Twenty seconds later he surfaces and slaps again. Warning shots, but what a great noise.

A few days later I walk north from Lake Street up Hoanjovo Lane following a tributary of the Nanny Hagen. Across the aqueduct and up the gulley to Bear Ridge Road. Here I meet Alan fixing the house he grew up in 50 years ago. I ask him the name of this stream. He tells me they called it the Brook. This fits with the name of the street to the south: Brook Manor. He recollects playing in the stream constantly as a child 50 years ago. "Back then there were lots of minnows, water striders and crayfish." And now? "Not so much … some frogs."

To the north of Colony Glen Road, the stream cuts through a gulley up to Bear Ridge Lake. This was developed as a small lake colony of vacation homes, but is now densely built out. The lake runs on a north-south axis and is fed by a small stream from Mountain Trail Park. This is another of the tiny Town of Mount Pleasant parks that ring the upper tributaries of the Nanny Hagen. It's a little green oasis, which of course is full of invasive phragmites. Nature is a mirror, but we're not looking.

Nine

Winter Returns

The other fork of the road — the one less traveled by — offers our last, our only chance to reach a destination that assures the preservation of the earth.

— Rachel Carson, *Silent Spring*

ENTERING THE SEASON of death and decay. The water continues to trickle through the swamp on this cool December morning. Little shards of ice at the edge. New ice cracks as it freezes on the pond. The lake speaks to the beaver and to me. The sky is wind wiped clear of clouds and smells of the frost-edged air. The circle of the year is closing. Soon the shortest day will be here.

I spend the beginning of December exploring the headwaters of the brook. Two streams run down from Old Farm Hill Park and the ridge between the Bronx River watershed in Armonk and the Nanny Hagen watershed. This ridge is the highest elevation for the stream at 610 feet above sea level.

A friend who lives up here shows me a front door video of a bobcat from a few nights ago. It's a big healthy girl: three to four feet long, with pointy ears, bobbed tail, and well-muscled. This is probably the same animal whose tracks I saw back in winter down at the aqueduct. These cats are strict carnivores and this one is out hunting. They are solitary, elusive animals; such a treat to see this one.

Hunting of bobcats used to be unregulated in New York and numbers were significantly reduced, but they are making a bit of a comeback here. Joshua DiPaola, Natural Resources Specialist from Rockefeller State Park Preserve, tells me that data from camera trap surveys indicate five different bobcats in the preserve. They have also been documented in adjacent Graham Hills Park.

I revisit with Dan Aitchison, Westchester Parks' curator of wildlife, to talk about the size of the bobcat population in Westchester. "We have no idea," says Dan. "These animals are only studied when they are trouble, such as deer, or when they are in trouble — when it's how many do we have left?" But he notes, "They're common, they're super common. It's just that they're elusive, so nobody knows they're here."

He recollects that one showed up in Chappaqua a couple of years back. "It made the newspapers and everyone was up in arms. 'It's going to eat my dogs!' But they've been here all along. That was the interesting thing with the pandemic, people were home and they suddenly started noticing things that were here all the time."

Nonetheless, bobcat populations are increasing. "Bobcats were completely extirpated from this area when it was all farmland," Dan says. That would be the 19th and early 20th century. Most certainly they are back here now and used to moving among human development.

I ask Dan what bobcats eat and learned that it is mostly rabbits and rodents. I've observed lots of cottontails along the aqueduct. He also notes, "They will take down deer. They do crazy stuff. If you see wounds on the neck, that's bobcat. They crush the trachea. Then they'll take big parts of the animal, stash it, and hide it with branches and leaves." This sounds like the Serengeti in Pleasantville.

Hunting is also down in Westchester. When Dan was a kid he remembers that a number of friends would run a line of traps and sell the fur for cash. That rarely happens anymore. Humans are not a threat now; we're more likely to be food resources with our trash.

It's great to see these animals returning. The hardest thing is to recognize that wildlife is wild. We need to adapt to the animals rather than have the animals adapt to us. The populations are expanding and the animals habituate to the people. Can we give them the room they need?

I follow deer trails from Old Farm Hill Park and across Deerfield Lane where the stream makes a rapid descent down to Munson Pond, considered the headwaters of Nanny Hagen Brook. This former farm pond is nestled into the upper reaches of the valley. Mown grass in backyards sweeps down to the pond. At the top of the valley sits another smaller pond. Both were used by the farm that was here, and are now used by the wildlife.

To the north the valley narrows, with steep woods on either side. It's a real challenge to climb up the western slope and to the top of the ridge. So quiet, so peaceful, tucked in here, with no human access; the place is reverting to wild.

A few days later I'm back in the woods north of Munson Pond. Here I come across a big 12-point white-tailed buck with his five does. What an impressive animal, the boss around here. Thick neck meeting solid square chest. Big legs and heavy rump. Golden tan hair except for a white patch under the chin. They bound off north.

On the top of the hill, black and blue cohosh. The slender wands which had white racemes in summer are all standing to attention. Dark blue berries turning paler in the silver light. Native Americans used this plant medicinally as a pain killer and sedative. A native highbush cranberry still has its bright red fruits adding lovely color to the stark brown landscape. These fruits will persist into deepest winter, critical sustenance for winter birds.

A steep descent brings me down to Bear Ridge Lake. To the north an old driveway parallel to a little stream that drains an old farm ice pond.

The cattails, phragmites and bulrushes are browning out to silver. The wind picks up and sends them swaying. The days shorten, the temperatures drop and the year comes full circle. A cardinal sings up, "Cheer, cheer; twee, twee, twee, twee, twee" and then she ends with the longer "tweee, tweee, tweee." They love this dense, shrubby edge space. All over it. To me, the soft, warm tan of the female is just as pretty as the bright male.

The little stream comes down from Apple Hill. To the east of the ridge, the water flows north to Tercia Brook and through Chappaqua to the Saw Mill River. Where I am standing the water flows south through Bear Ridge Lake to the Nanny Hagen Brook and then to the Saw Mill River. One foot either way and the water takes dramatically different routes to the same place. Such are the ups and downs of the hills here.

I spot bear prints in the mud on the track. Massachusetts bears are moving into this area. I'll come back over the next few days and see if I can get a sighting.

Brown leaves pile up against an old stone wall. The mist pulls in and distant trees, now bare, fade. The chill in the air keeps me moving. I follow the stream south, down the edge of Bear Ridge Lake, through the gulley, down Colony Glen Drive and along Robbins Road. This leads me back to the aqueduct; the stream goes under and

I go over. Down Hoanjovo Lane brings me and this little stream back to the Nanny Hagen Brook. A good hike.

Getting dark now in the late afternoon. The crescent moon hangs quietly in the southwestern sky with the setting sun behind. All reflected in the water. A stillness envelops the pond, the surrounding trees and me.

The earth turns cold. It will soon be too hard to dig into. Birds flee south, monarchs too. But what of the bees, the snakes, the frogs and our small mammals? Their thoughts turn to hibernation. Frogs will actually freeze; other small critters enter a state of torpor. It's happening now as the temperature plummets.

A light dusting of snow overnight. Bare branches coated pure and white, glistening in the morning sun. A quiet quilt has settled over the world. I am not the first out this early morning. Tracks reveal the fox has been by on her daily route.

Up on the ridge, a few days later, all the snow has melted as the temperature warms up. I spot bear scat. A large brown pile with red berries. Black bear are increasingly common around here. I talk to Budd Viverka, a local bear wildlife expert at Mianus River Gorge. He says, "Bear sightings were rare here 15 years ago. We would occasionally hear of a bee hive destroyed, or see a lone male. But in 2016 we started seeing them more often." That year and every year since he has seen a mother with cubs. So now they're breeding at the gorge in Northern Westchester. That also mirrors Dan Aitchison's experience at nearby Ward Pound Ridge.

These bears have moved into northeastern Westchester from northwestern Connecticut and western Massachusetts.

Bears need a good-sized contiguous undisturbed area in which to breed. We now have that in Ward Pound Ridge, over 4,300 acres, and Mianus River Gorge, nearly 1,000 acres, both about 15 miles northwest of here.

Cubs den with the mother for a whole year. Female cubs often stay and den with the mother another year. But the adolescent males get kicked out. So they move south. One came here.

Lone males travel long distances. Two hundred and fifty miles in two months. Habituation of bears is a big issue says Budd: "Don't feed the bears! A fed bear is a dead bear." We want these animals to stay wild, but as they come into human contact opportunities for trouble increase. As it's so late in the season, Budd thinks this male is probably denning in the area. I wonder if I'll see him again. Hope so.

So much has changed over the last 30 years that I've lived and walked this land. The four distinct seasons are now muddled. The winters are starting later and becoming milder. Spring is much longer. Warm nights in October mean leaf season is shorter and later. But the bigger mammals are coming back — joy. Eagles are returning too. In the 1950s only one bald eagle nested in the state; now we have over 400 nests.

Out late tonight. Glass-hard air and the stars close enough to hold. Everything black and silver in the moon-light. Crunch underfoot.

I spot fresh coyote scat in the cold morning. Brown, moist. Little hair. She ate well last night. A welcome change in the last few years has been the decreasing deer popula-tion. Perhaps they are being kept in check by the coyotes and bobcats. That would be a good thing.

The beaver has been busy. Two more trees felled and progress has been made on his dam. The chocolate reeds are disintegrating. Silver sun streams through. Goldenrods brown out. Sedges tan underneath as they die back. Still water. The quiet little refuge remains. Another year over.

Acknowledgments

I would like to thank the friends who joined me on my many walks: James Eyring, Helen Meurer, Eileen West, Willem Don, Elaine Sackman, and Steven Kavee. Gratitude to the experts I consulted: Andy Reinmann, Rebecca Policello, Michael Finewood, Dan Aitchison, Jim Nordgren, Joshua DiPaolo, Danielle Begley-Smith, Budd Viverka, and Chris Nagy. Any and all errors are mine. Thanks to my two editors, Elsbeth Lindner and Kim Inglis, and to my excellent designer Jonathan Gullery. Most of all, my gratitude goes to artist and illustrator GG Kopilak for her beautiful drawings which bring the book to life and to my wife, Suzanne, for her steadfast support.

Index of Species

Trees

Shrubs

Vines

Grasses, Sedges and Rushes

Wild Flowers and Herbs

Ferns

Fungi, Lichens and Mosses

Insects

Amphibians and Fish

Birds

www.ingramcontent.com/pod-product-compliance
Lightning Source LLC
Chambersburg PA
CBHW051128160726
47997CB00018B/816